OPPOSING VIEWPOINTS® SERIES

Performance-Enhancing Drugs

Other Books of Related Interest:

Opposing Viewpoints Series
Addiction
Dietary Supplements
Prescription Drug Abuse

At Issue Series
Club Drugs
Mexico's Drug War

Current Controversies Series
Drug Legalization
Prescription Drugs

"Congress shall make no law . . . abridging the freedom of speech, or of the press."

First Amendment to the US Constitution

The basic foundation of our democracy is the First Amendment guarantee of freedom of expression. The Opposing Viewpoints series is dedicated to the concept of this basic freedom and the idea that it is more important to practice it than to enshrine it.

OPPOSING VIEWPOINTS® SERIES

Performance-Enhancing Drugs

Roman Espejo, Book Editor

GREENHAVEN PRESS
A part of Gale, Cengage Learning

GALE
CENGAGE Learning·

Farmington Hills, Mich • San Francisco • New York • Waterville, Maine
Meriden, Conn • Mason, Ohio • Chicago

Patricia Coryell, *Vice President & Publisher, New Products & GVRL*
Douglas Dentino, *Manager, New Products*
Judy Galens, *Acquisitions Editor*

For more information, contact:
Greenhaven Press
27500 Drake Rd.
Farmington Hills, MI 48331-3535
Or you can visit our Internet site at gale.cengage.com

Articles in Greenhaven Press anthologies are often edited for length to meet page requirements. In addition, original titles of these works are changed to clearly present the main thesis and to explicitly indicate the author's opinion. Every effort is made to ensure that Greenhaven Press accurately reflects the original intent of the authors. Every effort has been made to trace the owners of copyrighted material.

Cover Image copyright © PhotoSGH/Shutterstock.com.

LIBRARY OF CONGRESS CATALOGING-IN-PUBLICATION DATA

Performance-enhancing drugs / Roman Espejo, book editor.
    pages cm. -- -- (Opposing viewpoints) Summary: "Opposing Viewpoints: Performance-Enhancing Drugs: Opposing Viewpoints is the leading source for libraries and classrooms in need of current-issue materials. The viewpoints are selected from a wide range of highly respected sources and publications"-- Provided by publisher.
    Includes bibliographical references and index.
    ISBN 978-0-7377-7280-7 (hardback) -- ISBN 978-0-7377-7281-4 (paperback)
    1. Doping in sports. I. Espejo, Roman, 1977- II. Title: Performance enhancing drugs.
    RC1230.P4762 2015
    362.29'088796--dc23
                                        2014030238

Printed in the United States of America
2 3 4 5 6   19 18 17 16 15

Contents

Chapter 3: How Effective Is Testing to Detect Performance-Enhancing Drugs?

Chapter 4: What Is the Future of Performance-Enhancing Drugs?

Why Consider Opposing Viewpoints?

> *"The only way in which a human being can make some approach to knowing the whole of a subject is by hearing what can be said about it by persons of every variety of opinion and studying all modes in which it can be looked at by every character of mind. No wise man ever acquired his wisdom in any mode but this."*
>
> *John Stuart Mill*

In our media-intensive culture it is not difficult to find differing opinions. Thousands of newspapers and magazines and dozens of radio and television talk shows resound with differing points of view. The difficulty lies in deciding which opinion to agree with and which "experts" seem the most credible. The more inundated we become with differing opinions and claims, the more essential it is to hone critical reading and thinking skills to evaluate these ideas. Opposing Viewpoints books address this problem directly by presenting stimulating debates that can be used to enhance and teach these skills. The varied opinions contained in each book examine many different aspects of a single issue. While examining these conveniently edited opposing views, readers can develop critical thinking skills such as the ability to compare and contrast authors' credibility, facts, argumentation styles, use of persuasive techniques, and other stylistic tools. In short, the Opposing Viewpoints Series is an ideal way to attain the higher-level thinking and reading skills so essential in a culture of diverse and contradictory opinions.

In addition to providing a tool for critical thinking, Opposing Viewpoints books challenge readers to question their own strongly held opinions and assumptions. Most people form their opinions on the basis of upbringing, peer pressure, and personal, cultural, or professional bias. By reading carefully balanced opposing views, readers must directly confront new ideas as well as the opinions of those with whom they disagree. This is not to argue simplistically that everyone who reads opposing views will—or should—change his or her opinion. Instead, the series enhances readers' understanding of their own views by encouraging confrontation with opposing ideas. Careful examination of others' views can lead to the readers' understanding of the logical inconsistencies in their own opinions, perspective on why they hold an opinion, and the consideration of the possibility that their opinion requires further evaluation.

Evaluating Other Opinions

To ensure that this type of examination occurs, Opposing Viewpoints books present all types of opinions. Prominent spokespeople on different sides of each issue as well as well-known professionals from many disciplines challenge the reader. An additional goal of the series is to provide a forum for other, less known, or even unpopular viewpoints. The opinion of an ordinary person who has had to make the decision to cut off life support from a terminally ill relative, for example, may be just as valuable and provide just as much insight as a medical ethicist's professional opinion. The editors have two additional purposes in including these less known views. One, the editors encourage readers to respect others' opinions—even when not enhanced by professional credibility. It is only by reading or listening to and objectively evaluating others' ideas that one can determine whether they are worthy of consideration. Two, the inclusion of such viewpoints encourages the important critical thinking skill of objectively evaluating an author's credentials and bias. This evaluation will illuminate an author's reasons for taking a particular stance on an issue and will aid in readers' evaluation of the author's ideas.

It is our hope that these books will give readers a deeper understanding of the issues debated and an appreciation of the complexity of even seemingly simple issues when good and honest people disagree. This awareness is particularly important in a democratic society such as ours in which people enter into public debate to determine the common good. Those with whom one disagrees should not be regarded as enemies but rather as people whose views deserve careful examination and may shed light on one's own.

Thomas Jefferson once said that "difference of opinion leads to inquiry, and inquiry to truth." Jefferson, a broadly educated man, argued that "if a nation expects to be ignorant and free . . . it expects what never was and never will be." As individuals and as a nation, it is imperative that we consider the opinions of others and examine them with skill and discernment. The Opposing Viewpoints series is intended to help readers achieve this goal.

David L. Bender and Bruno Leone,
Founders

Introduction

> "*Together with the rapidly increasing knowledge on genetic therapies as a promising new branch of regular medicine, the issue has arisen whether these techniques might be abused in the field of sports.*"
>
> —*H.J. Haisma and O. de Hon,* "*Gene Doping,*" International Journal of Sports Medicine, *April 27, 2006*

In 2003 the World Anti-Doping Agency (WADA) and the International Olympic Committee (IOC) included gene doping on their lists of banned substances and methods.

In its definition of gene doping, WADA makes its position clear: "The non-therapeutic use of cells, genes, genetic elements, or of the modulation of gene expression, having the capacity to enhance athletic performance, is prohibited." Gene doping draws from the science of gene therapy, in which DNA is transferred to a patient's cells to replace a mutated gene, disable it, or introduce a new gene to treat or prevent a disorder. In sports, it aims to modify existing genes or add one to the athlete's genetic makeup for a competitive edge. In the place of anabolic steroid injections, the gene that encodes the protein myostatin, which restricts the growth of muscle cells, could be inactivated to increase strength and muscle mass. To boost endurance, an extra copy of the gene that creates the hormone erythropoietin (EPO), which controls the production of red blood cells, could be given instead of EPO itself.

The allure of gene doping is that it could provide what makes an individual a "natural" at athletics while sidestepping the use of conventional performance-enhancing drugs (PEDs). "Genes have a cachet all their own. Some people are born genetically adept at strength sports, some at endurance sports," claims James Christie, sports reporter for the *Globe and Mail.* "Parents, trainers and corporate interests are on the genetic bandwagon." In fact, Christie cites Atlas Sports Genetics, which offers parents the chance to see if their children carry the ACTN3 gene, the "sports gene" purportedly found in elite athletes. Moreover, gene doping is more difficult to detect than synthetic substances. "The crux of the problem is that there is no difference between the product of an artificially introduced gene and one produced naturally in the athlete's own body," explains Nationale Anti-Doping Agentur (NADA) Austria. "Detecting doping with hormones, for instance with EPO, is possible because the molecular structure of natural, endogenous EPO differs from that of exogenous EPO (originating outside the body)," continues NADA Austria. "This is not possible with gene doping, because the athlete engaged in doping produces the doping substance in his or her own body." Other methods of testing may be pursued, such as performing a biopsy on a tissue sample or screening for abnormal gene activity. It is reported that the IOC intends to implement testing for gene doping at the 2016 Summer Olympics. "We will certainly, as soon as we have a reliable method available, make use of it for the purpose of identifying whether there is something going on based on strategic information," says Arne Ljungqvist, chairman of the committee's medical commission.

Gene doping allegations concerning Chinese swimmer Ye Shiwen surfaced at the 2012 Summer Olympics. The sixteen-year-old unknown won the gold in the women's 200-meter and 400-meter individual medley, breaking the Olympic record in the former and world record in the latter. Additionally, Ye beat her time in the 400-meter individual medley at the World Championships in 2011 by seven seconds and swam the final leg faster than American swimmer Ryan Lochte in the same event for men. "Any time someone has looked like superwoman in the history of our sport they have later been found guilty of doping," argues John Leonard, executive director of the World Swimming Coaches Association (WSCA). "To swim three other splits at the rate that she did, which was quite ordinary for elite competition, and then unleash a historic anomaly, it is just not right." He concludes that Ye, who had passed all drug tests, underwent genetic manipulation or some other form of performance enhancement.

On the other hand, not everyone believes that Ye's stunning victories are an anomaly explained only by performance enhancement. Wesley Stephenson, broadcast journalist at BBC News, contends that the swimmer's performance was not that unusual in the context of the sport's statistics. For example, Stephenson states that one of Ye's competitors, Australian swimmer Stephanie Rice, beat her best time by six seconds when she broke a world record in 2008. "Sport scientists say that during a teenage growth spurt, there is a release of hormones that can suddenly increase the powers of endurance," he proposes. As for Ye swimming faster than Lochte, Stephenson points out that he swam twenty-three seconds faster than her overall and had previously swam slower than a woman in the final leg of the 400 meter. "Lochte simply paced himself over the race very differently to Ye Shiwen," he persists.

The IOC defended Ye against the accusations, but it is speculated that the 2012 Summer Olympics may have been the last to be free of genetic enhancement. "Gene doping has been sort of smoldering as a theoretical possibility for at least two or three sets of Olympic Games," claims Theodore Friedmann, chairman of WADA's genetics panel. Furthermore, advances in current PEDs remain a robust challenge for professional sports and anti-doping organizations, particularly in the race for detection. *Opposing Viewpoints: Performance-Enhancing Drugs* investigates this topic and more in chapters titled "Should the Use of Performance-Enhancing Drugs Be Accepted?," "How Dangerous Are Performance-Enhancing Drugs?," "How Effective Is Testing to Detect Performance-

Enhancing Drugs?," and "What Is the Future of Performance-Enhancing Drugs?" The divergent and conflicting perspectives and analyses presented in this volume reinforce PEDs as a controversial presence in sports and a polarizing factor in realizing human potential.

Should the Use of Performance-Enhancing Drugs Be Accepted?

Chapter Preface

In 2013 former cyclist Lance Armstrong came clean about allegations of using performance-enhancing drugs (PEDs)—erythropoietin (EPO), human growth hormone (HGH), and testosterone—in addition to undergoing blood transfusions. "I didn't invent the culture, but I didn't try to stop the culture, and that's my mistake, and that's what I have to be sorry for," he said in a televised interview with Oprah Winfrey. Armstrong admitted to doping throughout his seven consecutive wins of the Tour de France, from 1999 to 2005, all of which have been stripped from Armstrong. "My ruthless desire to win at all costs served me well on the bike but the level it went to, for whatever reason, is a flaw," Armstrong explained.

Following his admission, whether he should be forgiven for his doping violations and lies filled the headlines. "I, for one, forgive Lance Armstrong for his trespasses," declares Andy Konty, a columnist for the Bleacher Report, a sports website. Konty praises Armstrong for his exceptional work ethic and willpower, in which he trained for his tours at least eight hours a day. "The PEDs cannot create these qualities. PEDs only enhance them," Konty maintains. In fact, Konty argues that Armstrong beat his competitors without an unfair advantage, as doping in cycling was the norm, not the exception. "Armstrong wasn't cheating. He was playing by the rules of the peloton."

However, others contend that Armstrong is beyond forgiveness as an athlete. "Each profession has its unforgivable sin, and in sports it is doping," writes Lauren Fleshman, a professional track-and-field runner, in an open letter to Armstrong. She contends that Armstrong's career contradicts the very meaning of athletic competition. "To you," Fleshman contends, "the most important thing in sports is winning. But the central tenet of being a professional athlete is not winning; it is fair play. In your warped world, everyone is a cheater, but in reality, 99% of us are doing it right." She believes that the only option for Armstrong to redeem himself is to never compete again: "You have an opportunity to do something noble tonight, Lance. Retire." In the following chapter, the authors deliberate whether the use of performance-enhancing drugs in sports should be accepted.

"Perhaps the wrongness of drugs in sports resides in nothing more than that it is against the rules."

The Use of Performance-Enhancing Drugs Is Cheating

Stephen Mumford

Stephen Mumford is a metaphysics professor and dean of the faculty of arts at the University of Nottingham in England. He is also the author of Watching Sport: Aesthetics, Ethics and Emotion. *In the following viewpoint, Mumford equates the choice to use performance-enhancing drugs (PEDs) to opting out of sports; it is not always a question of unfair advantages or protecting athletes. He argues that one must accept the preconditions of a game and inefficient means to achieve a goal—such as jumping over a bar instead of walking under it—or game playing is not possible. Breaking the rules of a sport by using drugs forfeits the preconditions of the game, he maintains, and breaks away from playing the sport for its own sake and instead playing for monetary gain or fame.*

As you read, consider the following questions:

1. How are ethical and aesthetic values connected in sports, according to Mumford?

2. Why are arguments against PEDs not always cut-and-dried, as claimed by the author?

3. What should be expected of game playing, as stated in the viewpoint?

Widespread moral outrage has been prompted by [former professional cyclist] Lance Armstrong finally coming clean on his use of performance-enhancing drugs in his sport. Some purchasers of his autobiography have demanded refunds on the grounds of the work being bought as fact that is now considered fiction. Armstrong was a cheat; and we feel cheated.

There is a good reason for this. Ethical and aesthetic values can be closely connected, as the case of sport illustrates. In *Watching Sport*, I argued that moral flaws can detract from the aesthetic value of sport, while moral virtues can increase it, and I used Lance Armstrong as one illustration. Back then, Armstrong fell into the latter category. The beauty of his victories was enhanced by his return from cancer. Now that we know there was a different kind of enhancement involved, the aesthetic is ruined. [Sprinter] Ben Johnson's 1988 Olympic sprint was similarly destroyed aesthetically by its basis in cheating.

Not Always Cut-and-Dried

If we assume that sporting beauty can be defeated by an ethical vice, we had better be sure that the use of drugs in sport really is wrong. While the judgments of sporting authorities are all or nothing—guilt or innocence—the arguments are not always so cut-and-dried. Chemicals in bodies come in degrees, and disqualifications do not. Some such chemicals are naturally occurring, such as testosterone. Up to a certain level, an athlete is innocent of wrongdoing. The slightest degree over the limit, and they bear absolute guilt. Might an athlete then try to get as close to the legal limit as they can, without exceeding it? Some other cases are claimed to have been a result of accidental ingestion of a drug, as in the case of British skier Alain Baxter, who was stripped of his 2002 Winter Olympic medal after the use of a shop-bought inhaler. And although the drug in his body was on the banned list, it was acknowledged to be an inactive variety of it. The drug had no performance-enhancing value. The wrongness of drug-cheating in sport does not, therefore, rest only on level-playing-field considerations or unfair advantage. And it is not always a question of protection of the athletes either. Some performance enhancers are damaging to health, but not all are. Maybe the harmless ones should be allowed.

Here is a different approach. Perhaps the wrongness of drugs in sport resides in nothing more than that it is against the rules. It's wrong because it's cheating. We want the rules obeyed, whatever they are, and some of those just happen to concern drug use. After all, some of the arguments above could apply to other cases of cheating in sport or violation of the rules. A snooker [the British game of pool] player cannot hope to escape sanction just because a hanging sleeve knocked a ball accidentally, and nor would it matter if the ball's movement was of no advantage. It's a foul either way. And in football, the ball can be taken as close to the boundary of play as one likes, but once it crosses that line—no matter how little—it is out of play absolutely. All or nothing calls are frequently essential in sport. At least the rules for drugs in sport are relatively clear.

Opting Out of the Sport

Why, though, would anyone knowingly cheat, even if they thought they could escape punishment? In one of the finest

Doping Is Akin to Death

Doping is cheating. Doping is akin to death. Death physiologically, by profoundly altering, sometimes irreversibly, normal processes through unjustified manipulations. Death physically, as certain tragic cases in recent years have shown. But also death spiritually and intellectually, by agreeing to cheat and conceal one's capabilities, by recognizing one's incapacity or unwillingness to accept oneself, or to transcend one's limits. And finally death morally, by excluding oneself de facto from the rules of conduct required by all human society.

Juan Antonio Samaranch,
Speech at the Olympic Museum,
Lausanne (Switzerland), 1998.

books in the philosophy of sport, [philosopher] Bernard Suits' *The Grasshopper*, the playing of games is defended as an end in itself. One plays for its own sake, and consequently we should expect game playing to be the centrepiece of any imagined utopia. It follows, argues Suits, that one accepts the rules of a game precisely because it is a precondition of the playing of the game. One accepts a *lusory* goal in sport, an inefficient means of achieving some task, precisely because without the constraint of rules, game playing would not be possible. Thus, one accepts that one has to jump over the bar, rather than walk under it; one has to run all the way around the track instead of cutting across the infield; and one has to get the ball in the hole by hitting it with a club instead of carrying it and dropping it in there. Some of these constraints are fairly arbitrary. Games can and do evolve in all sorts of ways. But unless one accepts those rules, one is not playing. You may get to the other side of the bar, but unless you have done so by jumping over it, you are not playing high jump. And similarly, it can be contended, if one breaks the rules of drug use, one has opted out of the sport.

Assuming that is right, what tempts someone like Armstrong to knowingly opt out of the sport? Why did he voluntarily stop competing in cycling? Indeed, why would anyone cut across the infield in a 400-metre race, even if they could do so undetected? And would they really have "won" the race if they did so? Arguably not. But if someone willingly stops playing, while adopting the appearance of playing, doesn't that show that something has gone wrong with sport? It is no longer befitting Suits' utopia. It is not being done for its own sake but, rather, for the rewards of finance and fame. In that case, something has gone wrong in society's institutionalisation of sport.

A Recipe for Cheating

And here is a more general lesson, for cheating does not occur only in sport. Academics are acutely aware of incidents of plagiarism. One website was found offering to write undergraduate essays, with a pricing scale determined by length and class of the essay. The same site even offered to write PhD theses, for a price. Why would anyone want to take up that offer? Why graduate knowing that it is not one's own achievement? Just like sport, learning should be its own reward. If we reach the point where the instrumental value of such achievements outweighs their intrinsic value, then we have created a defective society and a recipe for cheating.

> "Would the legalization and regulation
> of [performance-enhancing drugs] be a
> fair and safe way out?"

Performance-Enhancing Drugs Should Be Legalized

Stephen Wang

In the following viewpoint, Stephen Wang supports the legalization of performance-enhancing drugs (PEDs) in professional athletics. For instance, he insists that doping has become a necessity—and accepted—to win in numerous sports, with most of the top finishers in cycling found guilty of the practice. Additionally, testing for PEDs is exceedingly difficult for governing bodies, Wang states, as drug makers continue to develop undetectable substances and athletes engage in doping practices that allow them to avoid testing positive. Legalizing PEDs, he proposes, would reduce the health risks, deter criminal activity, and make more effective use of limited resources. The author is a reporter for the International, a news website.

As you read, consider the following questions:

1. In what ways are drugs designed to be undetectable by regulators, as told by Wang?

2. According to the viewpoint, what do Bengt Kayser and his colleagues state about medically supervising doping?

3. According to Wang, what threatens the biological passport for catching dopers?

The shocking revelation of performance-enhancing drug use by star athletes has been a repeating occurrence in the world of professional athletics. Most recently, the discovery that American sprinter, Tyson Gay and his Jamaican rival, Asafa Powell, used performance-enhancement drugs (PEDs) has raised questions about the efficacy of organizations such as the World Anti-Doping Agency (WADA) in enforcing clean athletic competition. The frequency of such discoveries, the seeming incapability of officials in catching drug users before major sporting events, as well as concerns over doping becoming an accepted practice in sports, has led some to consider a radical change: the legalization of PEDs.

Doping to Win: A Necessity Now?

From 1990 to now, over 240 top professional cyclists have been caught using PEDs, a practice known as doping. When asked by the French newspaper *Le Monde* if it was possible to win without doping, Lance Armstrong, seven time Tour de France winner, said, "That depends on which race you wanted to win. The Tour de France? No. Impossible to win without doping." For certain sports, especially those with a history of extensive PED usage by athletes, doping is seen as both necessary to remain competitive and an acceptable practice.

"I was part of a culture where it was white noise," said cyclist David Millar to CNN. Millar, who admitted to doping in 2004 and served a two-year suspension from professional competition, said, "It was something with a certain inevitability to it—if I ever wanted to be the best and be professional." Alarmingly, the necessity of using PEDs to become the best as

Millar described, has played out in major cycling races, with many of the top finishers later found guilty of doping.

In 1999, if all athletes eventually discovered of doping were removed, the winner of the Tour de France would have been the 7th place finisher according to the sports column Eurosport. In 2000, the winner would have been the 10th place finisher, 4th in 2001, 10th in 2002, 5th in 2003, and 8th in 2004 and 2005. More recent results are not definite since doping is usually discovered years later, but as the trend has shown, top finishers are usually those who dope.

A Difficult Task: Catching Dopers

The guarantee of a clean sport relies heavily upon the ability of regulating bodies to catch athletes who use PEDs. However, as former professional body builder and *Iron Man* magazine contributor Doug Brignole says, "Providing a guaranteed drug-free competitive arena is justifiable . . . though it's completely unrealistic at this point in time."

What researchers working on doping detection have known and what fans have been steadily becoming aware of is the advantage PED makers who develop newer, undetectable drugs have over the regulators who come up with tests to detect these drugs. In many cases, as Brignole describes, "[Agencies] are unable to stay ahead of the drug makers. They can only test for the 'markers' of drugs which have already been identified. A drug is undetectable until identified." Indeed, common detection methods such as urine and blood tests work by knowing the molecular structure of a drug and then testing for either the drug itself or its metabolites. Thus, if a chemist were to make a slight modification to the structure of a drug or if an athlete took a new, unidentified substance, tests would turn up negative. Similarly, other drugs leave behind nothing but an increase in substances that the body already produces naturally by itself.

Such was the case of the drug erythropoietin, commonly referred to as EPO, used by professional cyclists in the 1990s to boost red blood cell count. Not until 2001 was there a definitive test for detecting EPO. Consequently in the preceding decade, rampant use of the drug ensued. Of all the Tour de France jersey winners from 1992–2001, more than a dozen had either admitted to or were later revealed to be users of EPO. However, at the times of their victories, and for years afterwards, drug tests had shown up negative—in fact, some cyclists never actually tested positive but rather their usage was revealed through personal confessions. EPO, though now easily identifiable, represents the kind of drug skeptics of WADA and other anti-doping agencies worry about: drugs that are so new they have not been identified yet or those that do not yet have a definitive test for detection.

Aside from using newer, unidentified drugs, athletes also engage in other various doping techniques that are difficult to catch. Cyclists on blood doping drugs are known to draw out some of their own blood before a test, thereby decreasing red blood cell count down to legal levels, and then feeding the blood back into the body after the test. The list of practices that have been used and continue to be used successfully range from attaining false doctor's prescriptions for banned substances, to exploiting legal loopholes, to "low-tech" methods such as urine replacement.

In his book, *The Secret Race: Inside the Hidden World of the Tour de France: Doping, Cover-ups, and Winning at All Costs*, Tyler Hamilton, a former teammate of Lance Armstrong, recounts how cyclists exploited a law in Europe that prohibited testing at night, writing, "This means you can take anything you like, as long as it leaves your system in nine hours or less." With anti-doping agencies such as WADA lacking the authority to get around such laws, exploitative practices are bound to continue.

Zero Tolerance Will Always Fail

Doping will always be present in sport. A zero-tolerance approach will always fail. But so too will any policy which attempts to restrict access to performance-enhancing drugs and interventions in competitive sport. The question is what kind and how many failures will there be. We should choose the policy which best promotes the values of health, spectator interest, enforceability, fair competition and human excellence. That is a policy of regulated access to performance-enhancing drugs.

The zero-tolerance ban on drugs in sport is an example of the spectacular victory of ideology, wishful thinking, moralism and naivety over ethics and common sense. Human beings have limitations.

"The Armstrong Saga: Why We Should Legalise Performance Enhancing Drugs in Sport," Practical Ethics, 2013. www.practicalethics.ox.ac.uk.

"There is no way to detect in the human body the newer generation of technology products. The athletes have advisors who know how to use these substances and avoid detection ... [and they] have supporters who get them the latest drugs before they are even on the market," said Tapio Videman (MD, DMSci), the Heritage Senior Scholar of Rehabilitation Medicine at the University of Alberta, to Express News. "Either we change the methods of testing for this substance or give up testing completely."

How Would Legalized PEDs Work?

Though not every sport has a reputation for doping, some have called for the legalization of PEDs given the difficulty of catching drug users as well as the unfair advantages dopers have over their clean counterparts. It should be noted, however, that part of the reason some sports have a reputation for PEDs more than others is a result of more frequent testing. As noted by Brian Palmer of *Slate* in regard to cycling, "Cyclists get tested dozens of times per year—far more than other athletes."

With that said, arguments have been made to legalize and regulate PEDs. Similar to arguments made for the legalization and regulation of narcotics, arguments for the regulation of PEDs also point to a reduction of health risks, crime, and a better utilization of resources.

Regarding health risks and the purchase of drugs from criminal sources, Bennett Foddy, professor at Princeton University, says in a paper published in *Principles of Health Care Ethics*, "Because doping is illegal, the pressure is to make performance enhancers undetectable, rather than safe. Performance enhancers are produced or bought on the black market and administered in a clandestine, uncontrolled way with no monitoring of the athlete's health." The side effects of doping and the possibility of death as a result has long been an argument against the use of PEDs.

However, in a paper written in the *Lancet*, Professors Bengt Kayser, Alexandre Mauron, and Andy Miah write, "We believe that rather than drive doping underground, use of drugs should be permitted under medical supervision . . . by allowing medically supervised doping, the drugs used could be assessed for a clearer view of what is dangerous and what is not."

Furthermore, the paper looks into who bears the cost of anti-doping tests and organizations. "Elite athletes only represent a small fraction of the global population but the resources of anti-doping almost exclusively go into testing these athletes," says Kayser, Mauron, and Miah. They also point to how an increasing portion of funding for organizations such as WADA comes from governments and thus, also from taxpayers. In terms of practicality regarding spending of government money, especially for developing nations, the paper notes, "the priorities should lie elsewhere from a public health perspective."

But even with regulation limiting the health risks of doping, skeptics of legalization point to the ethical consequences of PEDs in terms of fairness and purity of sports. Michael J. Beloff, a British lawyer, says in the book *Drugs and Doping [in Sport: Socio-Legal Perspectives]*, "The objects of doping control are clear . . . a level playing field. . . . The use of drugs violates all such notions of equality: the drug taker starts with an unfair advantage."

However, Kayser, Mauron, and Miah argue that genetic predisposition already renders unfair advantages, given the fact that some people are naturally more fit than others. They point to three-time cross-country skiing gold medal winner Eero Mäntyranta who had a genetic mutation leading to naturally higher red blood cell counts. The question remains whether giving everyone, regardless of genetic advantages, access to PEDs would make a more level playing field. Would those who are naturally more fit benefit greater from doping than those who are not? Or are such doping benefits constrained by the natural limitations of the human body? Such answers are yet to be seen as more scientific research needs to be done.

In sports such as baseball that require skills other than just endurance, arguments have been made that strength-increasing drugs should not be banned. Gary Roberts, editor in chief of *Sports Lawyer*, says, "Home runs are hit only because the player has great skill at swinging a bat at a little ball coming at him at over 90 mph. Most folks . . . could take steroids all their lives and still not be able to hit that little ball," raising an interesting question of whether or not drugs that don't directly affect a player's game should be banned.

With some saying today's policies are inadequate in catching doping while also creating an environment of dangerous drug use, the idea of legalization and regulation of PEDs has gained some ground. But still, many sports fans yearn for the innocence of knowing their athletes are competing and winning fairly through hard work and dedication while also taking into account the unavoidable fact of genetic-given talent. A new promising anti-doping technique, known as a biological passport, is in the process of being implemented. The passport records athletes' biological markers collected over a period of time and compares new test results to previous records. Doping violations are detected when variances in certain biological markers exceed established limits. Implemented in 2008 by the Union Cycliste Internationale (UCI), the biological passport flagged 23 cyclists in its first year, according to the *Guardian*. Since then, the passport has seen some success in catching and sanctioning top cyclists such as Ivan Basso, former 3rd place Tour de France finisher, and Igor Astarloa, former champion of the road race world championships. Professional tennis has also added biological passports to its anti-doping procedures.

But even with a seemingly all-encompassing technique in place, rumors of a new type of doping threatens to overthrow the efficacy of the passport; genetic doping, the altering of genes, could provide athletes with a permanent and more natural-appearing advantage.

Such is the state of anti-doping today: When a breakthrough in detection is made, it is only to be met with newer roadblocks. It raises the question: Would the legalization and regulation of PEDs be a fair and safe way out?

"Elite spectator sports are supposed to be about the very best that humans can do, not the best drugs we can create."

Performance-Enhancing Drugs Should Not Be Legalized

Michael Rosenberg

In the following viewpoint, Michael Rosenberg argues that the legalization of performance-enhancing drugs (PEDs) would endanger athletes and undermine sports. Without a testing system in place for doping, athletes would be pressured to use steroids and other substances, Rosenberg claims, and this would place those who choose to stay clean at an inherent disadvantage. Moreover, while the use of PEDs would allow athletes to set new records, such accomplishments would be artificially—not humanly—achieved, he contends. Rosenberg is a writer for Sports Illustrated.

As you read, consider the following questions:

1. In Rosenberg's words, what would happen if PEDs were allowed?

2. What reasons does Rosenberg provide to explain why some athletes avoid PEDs?

3. What is Rosenberg's stance on the use of legal drugs in sports?

You know what sounds easy? Punting on the whole steroids issue. Give 'em all hypodermic needles with their signing bonuses. Let them pop pills. Let them inject pure, unfiltered testosterone. Let them eat uranium yellowcake if they think it will make them bigger, stronger, faster, quicker or better-looking.

You could do that. It would give sports journalists less work. It would theoretically make the games more fun (though I doubt it; more on that in a minute). It would allow [cyclist] Lance Armstrong to be an unquestioned hero, and it would save future Baseball Hall of Fame voters from making any moral judgments.

Of course, one day your son or daughter might be a professional athlete.

And all the other successful pro athletes will be juicing until their organs fall out, because they have no choice.

And your kid will figure: Hey, it's legal, and this is my only chance.

And then what?

Protecting the Innocent

The first goal of any legal system should be to protect the innocent. And I sure hope there will always be a place in popular sports for athletes who simply want to be their very best, naturally.

That is why sports need performance-enhancing drug testing. If you get rid of the testing, you punish those who are right so you can forgive those who are wrong.

Steroid use is not a victimless crime: There are only so many roster spots in each major sport, and the athletes who choose to stay clean are at an inherent disadvantage. And yes, some of them absolutely *do* choose to stay clean.

The fact is that people avoid drugs for all sorts of reasons: They're squares, they fear drugs will kill them, they don't want to get caught, they worry about their facial features and personality changing or a hundred other reasons. We all know performance-enhancing drugs are prominent in professional sports. It is the height of cynicism to say that literally everybody is doing it, or wants to.

Athletes, like any workers, have a right to believe their employers care about their health. Besides, a lot of the stuff on the banned substances lists is also illegal in this country. As a practical matter, you can't say it's OK to do something that the government says is illegal. What would happen then? If an NFL [National Football League] lineman gets arrested for steroid possession, would commissioner Roger Goodell suspend him for getting arrested but not for using steroids?

As for the stuff that is legal: that doesn't mean it's OK for everybody to ingest as much as they can. Some drugs have a medical purpose but are also performance-enhancing and dangerous if they are used in the wrong circumstance. (As a general rule, any baseball player who uses a female fertility drug should have to change diapers between innings.)

So this is not as simple as saying, "Hey, sports would be more entertaining if we just let everybody use steroids." There are serious ramifications for the people involved.

Also, who says sports would be more entertaining?

If steroids were totally legal, would somebody hit 80 home runs in a single season? Possibly. Would somebody break Usain Bolt's 100-meter record? Probably. But you know who could definitely break Bolt's record? A cheetah on amphetamines. So what?

Elite spectator sports are supposed to be about the very best that humans can do, not the best drugs we can create. One of the problems with the [baseball players] Mark

Why Sports Leaders Resign from the Fight Against Doping

Given such stakes, what might lead sports leaders to resign, however unconsciously, from the fight against doping? It is not so much the impact of big public scandals, as many people believe, nor the professional frustration of specialists in sports medicine and anti-doping inside sports organizations. Rather, in my observation, the chief threat turning doping into an unconsciously normalized practice for sports officers is the moral weathering and withering that result from the grinding everyday flow of discourse on drugs in sport. Information fatigue can render officials no longer able to perceive, with moral accuracy, what is right before their eyes.

John J. MacAloon, "Doping and Moral Authority: Sport Organizations Today," in Doping in Elite Sport: The Politics of Drugs in the Olympic Movement. *Eds. Wayne Wilson and Edward Derse. Champaign, IL: Human Kinetics, 2001.*

McGwire/Sammy Sosa home run races, in retrospect, is that they didn't even seem real then. They seemed like something [film director] George Lucas created.

At the time, that made McGwire and Sosa compelling. But if you knew then what you know now [McGwire and Sosa have both been linked to steroid use], would there be any thrill in watching them break Roger Maris' record [of 61 home runs in a single season]? Or would it all seem artificial—which, of course, it probably was?

Dunking from the foul line was mind-boggling when [basketball player] Julius Erving did it, but it's only mildly entertaining when the Phoenix Suns' Gorilla does it, because the

Gorilla uses a trampoline. Do we really want our best athletes to use pharmaceutical trampolines? Would that make this more fun?

A Very Different Experience

For all the talk about steroids in sports, the fact is that we never, ever absolutely KNOW that an athlete is on drugs when we watch live. Sometimes we guess and sometimes we're right. But I think this would be a very different experience if we knew they were all juicing.

It is pretty clear, at this point, that any public outrage about performance-enhancing drugs is selective outrage. People are outraged that [baseball player] Barry Bonds and his ever-expanding head obliterated the record book, because most Americans love baseball records and hate Barry Bonds. People are far more forgiving of [football players] Shawne Merriman and Julius Peppers and Rodney Harrison, because the NFL controls 10 percent of the average American's brain, and we figure what the hell, it's a violent sport, and does this really affect my fantasy team?

[Baseball player] Alex Rodriguez seems like a fraud, so when he (sort of) admits to steroid use, he gets ripped. But when A-Rod hit his 600th career home run, many people cheered. [Baseball player] Jason Giambi seems like a nice, easygoing dude, so when he (sort of) admits to steroid use, he gets forgiven.

Does this all make sense? Of course not. Sports are entertainment, and these guys are all cartoon characters to us.

But they aren't really cartoon characters. And I don't think we truly want them to be cartoon characters. We want humans to do superhuman things—but only in a very human way. Yes, you can try to make steroids legal. That doesn't mean they will ever seem OK.

> "What we are watching when we watch élite sports, then, is a contest among wildly disparate groups of people, who approach the starting line with an uneven set of genetic endowments and natural advantages."

Genetics Gives Athletes an Unfair Advantage

Malcolm Gladwell

Malcolm Gladwell is a Canadian journalist, author, and staff writer for the New Yorker. *In the following viewpoint, he asserts that athletes born with genetic advantages present a contradiction in maintaining the fairness of sports. It is a common story among elite athletes, Gladwell states; a champion cross-country skier carries a rare genetic mutation that significantly boosts his body's production of red blood cells—endowing him abnormal endurance—and the evolutionary physical characteristics of Kenyan and Ethiopian long-distance runners make them the best in the world. Surgical procedures are accepted as a means to improve athletes' abilities and training, but the use of performance-enhancing drugs (PEDs) to mimic the genetic advantages of others remains contentious, he observes.*

As you read, consider the following questions:

1. What advantages was Donald Thomas born with that optimized him for the high jump, as told by Gladwell?

2. How does addressing the natural inequalities in academics differ from sports, according to Gladwell?

3. What is the author's position on Lance Armstrong's doping scandal?

Toward the end of *The Sports Gene*, David Epstein makes his way to a remote corner of Finland to visit a man named Eero Mäntyranta. Mäntyranta lives in a small house next to a lake, among the pine and spruce trees north of the Arctic Circle. He is in his seventies. There is a statue of him in the nearby village. "Everything about him has a certain width to it," Epstein writes. "The bulbous nose in the middle of a softly rounded face. His thick fingers, broad jaw, and a barrel chest covered by a red knit sweater with a stern-faced reindeer across the middle. He is a remarkable-looking man." What's most remarkable is the color of his face. It is a "shade of cardinal, mottled in places with purple," and evocative of "the hue of the red paint that comes from this region's iron-rich soil."

Mäntyranta carries a rare genetic mutation. His DNA has an anomaly that causes his bone marrow to overproduce red blood cells. That accounts for the color of his skin, and also for his extraordinary career as a competitive cross-country skier. In cross-country skiing, athletes propel themselves over distances of ten and twenty miles—a physical challenge that places intense demands on the ability of their red blood cells to deliver oxygen to their muscles. Mäntyranta, by virtue of his unique physiology, had something like sixty-five per cent more red blood cells than the normal adult male. In the 1960, 1964, and 1968 Winter Olympic Games, he won a total of seven medals—three golds, two silvers, and two bronzes—and in the same period he also won two world-championship victories in the thirty-kilometre race. In the 1964 Olympics, he beat his closest competitor in the fifteen-kilometre race by forty seconds, a margin of victory, Epstein says, "never equaled in that event at the Olympics before or since."

Far Ahead of Ordinary Athletes

In *The Sports Gene*, there are countless tales like this, examples of all the ways that the greatest athletes are different from the rest of us. They respond more effectively to training. The shape of their bodies is optimized for certain kinds of athletic activities. They carry genes that put them far ahead of ordinary athletes.

Epstein tells the story of Donald Thomas, who on the seventh high jump of his life cleared 7'3.25"—practically a world-class height. The next year, after a grand total of eight months of training, Thomas won the world championships. How did he do it? He was blessed, among other things, with unusually long legs and a strikingly long Achilles tendon—ten and a quarter inches in length—which acted as a kind of spring, catapulting him high into the air when he planted his foot for a jump. (Kangaroos have long tendons as well, Epstein tells us, which is what gives them their special hop.)

Why do so many of the world's best distance runners come from Kenya and Ethiopia? The answer, Epstein explains, begins with weight. A runner needs not just to be skinny but—more specifically—to have skinny calves and ankles, because every extra pound carried on your extremities costs more than a pound carried on your torso. That's why shaving even a few ounces off a pair of running shoes can have a significant effect. Runners from the Kalenjin tribe, in Kenya—where the majority of the country's best runners come from—turn out to be skinny in exactly this way. Epstein cites a study comparing Kalenjins with Danes; the Kalenjins were shorter and had longer legs, and their lower legs were nearly a *pound* lighter.

That translates to eight per cent less energy consumed per kilometre. (For evidence of the peculiar Kalenjin lower leg, look up pictures of the great Kenyan miler Asbel Kiprop, a tall and elegant man who runs on what appear to be two ebony-colored pencils.) According to Epstein, there's an evolutionary explanation for all this: hot and dry environments favor very thin, long-limbed frames, which are easy to cool, just as cold climates favor thick, squat bodies, which are better at conserving heat.

Distance runners also get a big advantage from living at high altitudes, where the body is typically forced to compensate for the lack of oxygen by producing extra red blood cells. Not *too* high up, mind you. In the Andes, for example, the air is too rarefied for the kind of workouts necessary to be a world-class runner. The optimal range is six to nine thousand feet. The best runners in Ethiopia and Kenya come from the ridges of the Rift Valley, which, Epstein writes, are "plumb in the sweet spot." When Kenyans compete against Europeans or North Americans, the Kenyans come to the track with an enormous head start.

The Fantastic Menagerie of Human Biological Diversity

What we are watching when we watch élite sports, then, is a contest among wildly disparate groups of people, who approach the starting line with an uneven set of genetic endowments and natural advantages. There will be Donald Thomases who barely have to train, and there will be Eero Mäntyrantas, who carry around in their blood, by dumb genetic luck, the ability to finish forty seconds ahead of their competitors. Élite sports supply, as Epstein puts it, a "splendid stage for the fantastic menagerie that is human biological diversity." The menagerie is what makes sports fascinating. But it has also burdened high-level competition with a contradiction. We want sports to be fair and we take elaborate measures to make sure that no one competitor has an advantage over any other. But how can a fantastic menagerie ever be a contest among equals?

During the First World War, the U.S. Army noticed a puzzling pattern among the young men drafted into military service. Soldiers from some parts of the country had a high incidence of goitre—a lump on their neck caused by the swelling of the thyroid gland. Thousands of recruits could not button the collar of their uniform. The average I.Q. of draftees, we now suspect, also varied according to the same pattern. Soldiers from coastal regions seemed more "normal" than soldiers from other parts of the country.

The culprit turned out to be a lack of iodine. Iodine is an essential micronutrient. Without it, the human brain does not develop normally and the thyroid begins to enlarge. And in certain parts of the United States in those years there wasn't enough iodine in the local diet. As the economists James Feyrer, Dimitra Politi, and David Weil write, in a recent paper for the National Bureau of Economic Research:

> Ocean water is rich in iodine, which is why endemic goiter is not observed in coastal areas. From the ocean, iodine is transferred to the soil by rain. This process, however, only reaches the upper layers of soil, and it can take thousands of years to complete. Heavy rainfall can cause soil erosion, in which case the iodine-rich upper layers of soil are washed away. The last glacial period had the same effect: iodine-rich soil was substituted by iodine-poor soil from crystalline rocks. This explains the prevalence of endemic goiter in regions that were marked by intense glaciation, such as Switzerland and the Great Lakes region.

After the First World War, the U.S. War Department published a report called "Defects Found in Drafted Men," which detailed how the incidence of goitre varied from state to state, with rates forty to fifty times as high in places like Idaho, Michigan, and Montana as in coastal areas.

The story is not dissimilar from Epstein's account of Kenyan distance runners, in whom accidents of climate and geography combine to create dramatic differences in abilities. In the early years of the twentieth century, the physiological development of American children was an example of the "fantastic menagerie that is human biological diversity."

In this case, of course, we didn't like the fantastic menagerie. In 1924, the Morton Salt company, at the urging of public-health officials, began adding iodine to its salt, and initiated an advertising campaign touting its benefits. That practice has been applied successfully in many developing countries in the world: iodine supplementation has raised I.Q. scores by as much as thirteen points—an extraordinary increase. The iodized salt in your cupboard is an intervention in the natural order of things. When a student from the iodine-poor mountains of Idaho was called upon to compete against a student from iodine-rich coastal Maine, we thought of it as our moral obligation to redress their natural inequality. The reason debates over élite performance have become so contentious in recent years, however, is that in the world of sport there is little of that clarity. What if those two students were competing in a race? Should we still be able to give the naturally disadvantaged one the equivalent of iodine? We can't decide.

Epstein tells us that baseball players have, as a group, remarkable eyesight. The ophthalmologist Louis Rosenbaum tested close to four hundred major- and minor-league baseball players over four years and found an average visual acuity of about 20/13; that is, the typical professional baseball player can see at twenty feet what the rest of us can see at thirteen feet. When Rosenbaum looked at the Los Angeles Dodgers, he found that half had 20/10 vision and a small number fell below 20/9, "flirting with the theoretical limit of the human eye," as Epstein points out. The ability to consistently hit a baseball thrown at speeds approaching a hundred miles an hour, with a baffling array of spins and curves, requires the kind of eyesight commonly found in only a tiny fraction of the general population.

Drawing the Line at Drugs

Eyesight can be improved—in some cases dramatically—through laser surgery or implantable lenses. Should a promising young baseball player cursed with normal vision be allowed to get that kind of corrective surgery? In this instance, Major League Baseball says yes. Major League Baseball also permits pitchers to replace the ulnar collateral ligament in the elbow of their throwing arm with a tendon taken from a cadaver or elsewhere in the athlete's body. Tendon-replacement surgery is similar to laser surgery: It turns the athlete into an improved version of his natural self.

But when it comes to drugs, Major League Baseball—like most sports—draws the line. An athlete cannot use a drug to become an improved version of his natural self, even if the drug is used in doses that are not harmful, and is something that—like testosterone—is no more than a copy of a naturally occurring hormone, available by prescription to anyone, virtually anywhere in the world.

Baseball is in the middle of one of its periodic doping scandals, centering on one of the game's best players, Alex Rodriguez. Rodriguez is among the most disliked players of his generation. He tried to recover from injury and extend his career through illicit means. (He has appealed his recent suspension, which was based on these allegations.) It is hard to think about Rodriguez, however, and not think about Tommy John, who, in 1974, was the first player to trade in his ulnar collateral ligament for an improved version. John used modern medicine to recover from injury and extend his career. He won a hundred and sixty-four games after his transformation, far more than he did before science intervened. He had one of the longest careers in baseball history, retiring at the age of forty-six. His bionic arm enabled him to win at least twenty games a season, the benchmark of pitching excellence. People loved Tommy John. Maybe Alex Rodriguez looks at Tommy John—and at the fact that at least a third of current major-league pitchers have had the same surgery—and is genuinely baffled about why baseball has drawn a bright moral line between the performance-enhancing products of modern endocrinology and those offered by orthopedics.

The other great doping pariah is Lance Armstrong. He apparently removed large quantities of his own blood and then re-infused himself before competition, in order to boost the number of oxygen-carrying red blood cells in his system. Armstrong wanted to be like Eero Mäntyranta. He wanted to match, through his own efforts, what some very lucky people already do naturally and legally. Before we condemn him, though, shouldn't we have to come up with a good reason that one man is allowed to have lots of red blood cells and another man is not?

"I've always said you could have hooked us up to the best lie detectors on the planet and asked us if we were cheating, and we'd have passed," Lance Armstrong's former teammate Tyler Hamilton writes in his autobiography, *The Secret Race*. "Not because we were delusional—we knew we were breaking the rules—but because we didn't think of it as cheating. It felt fair to break the rules."

What If You Aren't Eero Mäntyranta?

The Secret Race deserves to be read alongside *The Sports Gene*, because it describes the flip side of the question that Epstein explores. What if you aren't Eero Mäntyranta?

Hamilton was a skier who came late to cycling, and he paints himself as an underdog. When he first met Armstrong—at the Tour DuPont, in Delaware—he looked around at the other professional riders and became acutely conscious that he didn't look the part. "You can tell a rider's fitness by the shape of his ass and the veins in his legs, and these asses were bionic, smaller and more powerful than any I'd ever seen," he writes. The riders' "leg veins looked like highway maps. Their arms were toothpicks. . . . They were like race-horses." Hamilton's trunk was oversized. His leg veins did not pop. He had a skier's thighs. His arms were too muscled, and he pedalled with an ungainly "potato-masher stroke."

When Hamilton joined Armstrong on the U.S. Postal Service racing team, he was forced to relearn the sport, to leave behind, as he puts it, the romantic world "where I used to climb on my bike and simply hope I had a good day." The makeover began with his weight. When Michele Ferrari, the key Postal Service adviser, first saw Hamilton, he told him he was too fat, and in cycling terms he was. Riding a bicycle quickly is a function of the power you apply to the pedals divided by the weight you are carrying, and it's easier to reduce the weight than to increase the power. Hamilton says he would come home from a workout, after burning thousands of calories, drink a large bottle of seltzer water, take two or three sleeping pills—and hope to sleep through dinner and, ideally, breakfast the following morning. At dinner with friends, Hamilton would take a large bite, fake a sneeze, spit the food into a napkin, and then run off to the bathroom to dispose of it. He knew that he was getting into shape, he says, when his skin got thin and papery, when it hurt to sit down on a wooden chair because his buttocks had disappeared, and when his jersey sleeve was so loose around his biceps that it flapped in the wind. At the most basic level, cycling was about physical transformation: It was about taking the body that nature had given you and forcibly changing it.

"Lance and Ferrari showed me there were more variables than I'd ever imagined, and they all mattered: wattages, cadence, intervals, zones, joules, lactic acid, and, of course, hematocrit," Hamilton writes. "Each ride was a math problem: a precisely mapped set of numbers for us to hit. . . . It's one thing to go ride for six hours. It's another to ride for six hours following a program of wattages and cadences, especially when those wattages and cadences are set to push you to the ragged edge of your abilities."

The Paradox of Endurance Sports

Hematocrit, the last of those variables, was the number they cared about most. It refers to the percentage of the body's blood that is made up of oxygen-carrying red blood cells. The higher the hematocrit, the more endurance you have. (Mäntyranta had a very high hematocrit.) The paradox of endurance sports is that an athlete can never work as hard as he wants, because if he pushes himself too far his hematocrit will fall. Hamilton had a natural hematocrit of forty-two per cent—which is on the low end of normal. By the third week of the Tour de France, he would be at thirty-six per cent, which meant a six per cent decrease in his power—in the force he could apply to his pedals. In a sport where power differentials of a tenth of a per cent can be decisive, this "qualifies as a deal breaker."

For the members of the Postal Service squad, the solution was to use the hormone EPO [erythropoietin] and blood transfusions to boost their hematocrits as high as they could without raising suspicion. (Before 2000, there was no test for EPO itself, so riders were not allowed to exceed a hematocrit of fifty per cent.) Then they would add maintenance doses over time, to counteract the deterioration in their hematocrit caused by races and workouts. The procedures were precise and sophisticated. Testosterone capsules were added to the mix to aid recovery. They were referred to as "red eggs." EPO (aka erythropoietin), a naturally occurring hormone that increases the production of red blood cells, was Edgar—short for Edgar Allan Poe. During the Tour de France, and other races, bags of each rider's blood were collected in secret locations at predetermined intervals, then surreptitiously ferried from stage to stage in refrigerated containers for strategic transfusions. The window of vulnerability after taking a drug—the interval during which doping could be detected—was called "glowtime." Most riders who doped (and in the Armstrong era, it now appears, nearly all the top riders did) would take two thousand units of Edgar subcutaneously every couple of days, which meant they "glowed" for a dangerously long time. Armstrong and his crew practiced microdosing, taking five hundred units of Edgar nightly and injecting the drug directly into the vein, where it was dispersed much more quickly.

Not a Magical Boost

The Secret Race is full of paragraphs like this:

> The trick with getting Edgar in your vein, of course, is that you have to get it *in* the vein. Miss the vein—inject it in the surrounding tissue—and Edgar stays in your body far longer, you might test positive. Thus, microdosing requires a steady hand and a good sense of feel, and a lot of practice; you have to sense the tip of the needle piercing the wall of the vein, and draw back the plunger to get a little bit of blood so you know you're in. In this, as in other things, Lance was blessed: he had veins like water mains. Mine were small, which was a recurring headache.

Hamilton was eventually caught and was suspended from professional cycling. He became one of the first in his circle to implicate Lance Armstrong, testifying before federal investigators and appearing on *60 Minutes*. He says that he regrets his years of using performance-enhancing drugs. The lies and duplicity became an unbearable burden. His marriage fell apart. He sank into a depression. His book is supposed to serve as his apology. At that task, it fails. Try as he might—and sometimes he doesn't seem to be trying very hard—Hamilton cannot explain why a sport that has no problem with the voluntary induction of anorexia as a performance-enhancing measure is so upset about athletes infusing themselves with their own blood.

"Dope is not really a magical boost as much as it is a way to control against declines," Hamilton writes. Doping meant that cyclists finally could train as hard as they wanted. It was the means by which pudgy underdogs could compete with natural wonders. "People think doping is for lazy people who want to avoid hard work," Hamilton writes. For many riders, the opposite was true:

> EPO granted the ability to suffer more; to push yourself farther and harder than you'd ever imagined, in both training and racing. It rewarded precisely what I was good at: having a great work ethic, pushing myself to the limit and past it. I felt almost giddy: this was a new landscape. I began to see races differently. They weren't rolls of the genetic dice, or who happened to be on form that day. They didn't depend on who you were. They depended on *what you did*—how hard you worked, how attentive and professional you were in your preparation.

This is a long way from the exploits of genial old men living among the pristine pines of northern Finland. It is a vision of sports in which the object of competition is to use science, intelligence, and sheer will to conquer natural difference. Hamilton and Armstrong may simply be athletes who regard this kind of achievement as worthier than the gold medals of a man with the dumb luck to be born with a random genetic mutation.

> *"To buy into genetic determinism in sport, to use that as the basis of rationalizing risky, pharmacological glory, is a dangerous mistake."*

Using Genetic Advantages for Athletes to Justify Performance-Enhancing Drugs Is Flawed

Leigh Cowart

In the following viewpoint, Leigh Cowart asserts that justifying the use of performance-enhancing drugs (PEDs) to compensate for genetic differences among athletes is dangerous. For instance, supporting the practice of blood doping to mimic poly-cythemia—a condition advantageous in endurance sports—ignores the life-threatening risks, cyclists' sudden deaths, and health hazards of polycythemia itself, she contends. Rationalizing the nonclinical use of testosterone and human growth hormone on the basis that they naturally occur in the body, Cowart continues, fails to account for the known side effects and unknown long-term consequences. These justifications, the author maintains, reflect narcissistic entitlement and disregard the dangers of PEDs to all athletes. Cowart is a writer and former editor at NSFWCORP, a digital newsmagazine.

As you read, consider the following questions:

1. According to the author, what does Malcolm Gladwell not recognize about health care access for athletes?

2. Why is it profoundly narcissistic to say that people are entitled to others' genetic advantages, in Cowart's opinion?

3. How does the use of anabolic steroids adversely affect other athletes in contact sports, as claimed by the author?

I first read "Man and Superman", [journalist and author] Malcolm Gladwell's piece on performance-enhancing drugs, at two in the morning. Unable to sleep, I was slumped on the couch stumbling through the Internet in the hope that my reclined position and mounting sleep debt would gradually overpower a small, glowing screen full of text.

It did not. Barely a quarter of the way through the piece, sleep was out of the question. My hackles raised in resolute response to this glittering turd of ethically reprehensible journalism.

Flushed and fuming, I tore through the article once, twice, again and again. Blood pressure rising, I angrily emailed my colleagues, unable to contain my horrified indignation. Clusters of frustration and abhorrence bombed my insomniac brain, and I fought the urge to wake my sleeping husband, to howl with him at the sheer absurdity of it all. Because to read Gladwell's "Man and Superman" is to be completely misled.

Gladwell cherry-picks his way through the complicated fields of physiology, genetics, and sport to frame an argument that is not only ill-informed, it's downright dangerous.

A Rosy Portrait of Pharmaceutical Enhancements

His argument? Performance-enhancing drugs make sports fairer. Based on the premise that genetic differences make athletic competitions inherently unfair, he argues that athletes should be allowed to use substances to compensate for these differences. Not only that, he even suggests that it is perhaps more commendable to use pharmaceuticals than it is to be born "lucky."

> What we are watching when we watch élite sports, then, is a contest among wildly disparate groups of people, who approach the starting line with an uneven set of genetic endowments and natural advantages.

Riffing off of the book *The Sports Gene*, and completely casting aside the 10,000 Hour Rule espoused in his best seller, *Outliers*, Gladwell makes the case that if one person has a genetic advantage, shouldn't everyone be allowed to cheat?

> We want sports to be fair and we take elaborate measures to make sure that no one competitor has an advantage over any other. But how can a fantastic menagerie ever be a contest among equals?

The use of performance-enhancing drugs presents the chance to explore an interesting ethical dilemma. The problem, however, is in Gladwell's omissions. His piece paints a rosy portrait of pharmaceutical enhancements. He likens them to the adoption of iodized salt. It has all the context of a sales pitch.

What Gladwell fails to mention—*at all*—are the risks involved in using performance-enhancing drugs. There is nothing about the risks of blood doping or of pharmaceutical enhancement. He even skips the risks inherent in the very genetic condition he holds up as "lucky." There is no mention of contact sports, where the decision to illegally enhance could be the difference between life and death for your competitor. There is no recognition that health care access for athletes is a continuum with the Lance Armstrongs at the upper end, with their elite teams of morally questionable medical practitioners, and with some kid at the bottom end, desperate for a place on the team, taking injectables that he gets from a friend of a friend. . . .

That Gladwell can proclaim the moral superiority of performance enhancement with no mention of the enormous physical toll that these drugs exact is f------ outrageous. Athletes are already testing the fringes of bodily limitations. Our blood, our hormones, our entire physical systems exist within certain parameters because those are limits that allow everything to work properly. Those limits keep us alive. So yes, of course it's f------ dangerous to screw around with that shit. Of course there are consequences. People die.

In "Doping and the Story of Those We Love," celebrated cyclist Greg LeMond and his wife, Kathy, share the harrowing story of Johannes Draaijer, a talented cyclist and newlywed who died of heart failure in his sleep. His wife, Anna-Lisa, woke up in the dead of night only to realize that she was sleeping next to the corpse of her beloved. Upon this horrifying discovery, she called Kathy, screaming into the phone with blood-chilling sorrow, "'He's dead! He is cold, he is cold. I am so afraid! Oh my God, oh my God!'"

An autopsy showed that Draaijer died with the shredded heart of a 70-year-old man. He was 27.

A Winning Genetic Lottery Ticket?

Nestled in the heart of Gladwell's defense of performance-enhancing drugs is Finnish skier Eero Mäntyranta. A decorated Olympian and world champion, Mäntyranta is perhaps best known—at least, in certain circles—for his blood. Namely, that his body makes too much of it.

See, Mäntyranta has a genetic mutation, primary familial and congenital polycythemia (PCFP), that causes his body to overproduce red blood cells. This increases his body's endogenous ability to oxygenate its tissues, which is a big competitive advantage for an endurance athlete. So much so, that people strive to achieve those results artificially. Of the three components of aerobic capacity—maximum cardiac output, maximum oxygen extraction, and hemoglobin mass—only hemoglobin mass can be well manipulated. And that's where blood doping comes in.

Gladwell frames Mäntyranta's genetic mutation as natural doping, making the case that since Mäntyranta's blood is naturally more red blood cell dense, allowing other athletes to dope only makes things fairer. It isn't technically wrong to call PCFP a kind of natural doping. What is wrong is the characterization of PCFP as a winning genetic lottery ticket. Aside from the fact that having extra blood doesn't actually do the work of training, sufferers of PCFP face serious risks.

Clinical symptoms of PCFP range from headaches, dizziness, and nosebleeds to thrombotic and hemorrhagic events: that's clots and bleeds, strokes and heart attacks. And then there's the weird symptom of extreme itching after bathing. The symptoms can be relieved by phlebotomy—literally, bloodletting. However, even if they reduce the hematocrit (volume of red blood cells in blood), patients still have a risk of cardiovascular morbidity and mortality.

But Gladwell doesn't bother mentioning the dangers that accompany such "dumb genetic luck". And later, when he writes about EPO and blood doping, he doesn't discuss all the cyclists who died in their sleep, their blood as thick as honeyed ketchup.

The Sludge Factor

The reason PCFP is dangerous—and doping even more so—comes down to the limits of physiology: the sludge factor. Millions of years of evolution have resulted in whole blood that is (a) liquid and flows easily and (b) of a viscosity that the heart is accustomed to pumping. To overly simplify, blood

55

doping is like turning your blood into molasses and asking your heart to keep up, all the while hoping that the sludge doesn't get stuck anywhere.

The sludge factor, known as hyperviscosity syndrome, puts endurance athletes at even greater risk. To withstand dehydration, their bodies hold on to more fluids at rest. This alone would be beneficial to someone with an artificially boosted hematocrit, as it would liquidate the sludge and keep resting hematocrit levels low. However, for well-conditioned athletes, fluid losses are increased during exercise. An athlete starting with a boosted hematocrit at rest could very quickly move into the critical sludge zone.

Consider Johan Sermon, the promising Belgian cyclist who went to bed early in preparation for an eight-hour training ride. The team doctor had recently given him a complete cardiac evaluation and found him to be in an excellent condition. But his own mother found him dead in the morning. Heart failure.

Or maybe you've heard of the sixteen-year-old cyclist named Marco Ceriani? He had a heart attack during a race, after which he slipped into a coma and died. Fabrice Salanson? He settled into sleep in preparation for the Tour of Germany. His teammate awoke to find that he'd died in his sleep. Heart attack.

The list goes on: from January 2003 to February 2004, eight cyclists died of heart attacks. Compare that to how Gladwell talks about EPO [erythropoietin], a chemical form of blood doping that triggers the body to make extra red blood cells, pulling a quote from *The Secret Race* by cyclist Tyler Hamilton to frame his argument: "People think doping is for lazy people who want to avoid hard work," Hamilton writes. For many riders, the opposite was true:

> "EPO granted the ability to suffer more; to push yourself farther and harder than you'd ever imagined, in both training and racing. It rewarded pre-

cisely what I was good at: having a great work ethic, pushing myself to the limit and past it. I felt almost giddy: this was a new landscape. I began to see races differently. They weren't rolls of the genetic dice, or who happened to be on form that day. They didn't depend on who you were. They depended on what you did—how hard you worked, how attentive and professional you were in your preparation."

It is a vision of sports in which the object of competition is to use science, intelligence, and sheer will to conquer natural difference. Hamilton and Armstrong may simply be athletes who regard this kind of achievement as worthier than the gold medals of a man with the dumb luck to be born with a random genetic mutation.

It is one thing to write a compelling sales pitch, but journalism requires context.

Doping has killed people during races, leaving parties, at the dentist, in their beds. The excess of iron it produces can cause liver problems, including cancer. Bodies, inundated with repeated injections of synthetic EPO, risk the development of antibodies to erythropoietin, resulting in debilitating anemia as the body tries to fight the protein hormone responsible for triggering the production of red blood cells. And all the while there's a heart straining under the sludge.

Bodies and Limits

It is profound narcissism that says we all are entitled to the perceived specialness granted to others. What would we say of Mäntyranta if he hadn't been a famous athlete? Who would want ketchup blood and purple, mottled skin? If you're going to make the argument that iodized salt is a performance-enhancing drug that evens the playing field, shouldn't we talk about ending global starvation and providing basic health care to all? Who is deciding the levels at which the playing fields of genetics, sport, life are considered *fair*?

Just look at this insidious horseshit:

> An athlete cannot use a drug to become an improved version of his natural self, even if the drug is used in doses that are not harmful, and is something that—like testosterone—is no more than a copy of a naturally occurring hormone, available by prescription to anyone, virtually anywhere in the world.

This phrasing is incredibly misleading. We cannot accurately judge the safety of drugs used off-label to enhance performance because testing them in such a way would be highly unethical and dangerous. The side effects that we do understand are known because of patients who take the drugs on a clinically necessary basis. Take for example, human growth hormone; it's used to treat exceptionally small stature in children, and we know that too much of it can result in the symptoms of acromegaly, like large heads, hands, feet, and organs. But excessive human growth hormone in a healthy, active adult? How much is safe? What's all the growth hormone going to be doing in there? How might this backfire?

And don't even get me started on "naturally occurring." Of course steroids are naturally occurring. Your body is making anabolic steroids right now. In fact, your body is making all manner of chemicals. But chances are it's making the correct amount. Remember that whole thing about bodies and limits?

Amplifying the Dangers of Contact Sports

But still, to focus only on the narcissism of entitlement is to miss the much bigger, more nefarious issue with performance-enhancing drugs. Athletes don't boost performance past normal human limits in a vacuum: Their actions affect their competitors.

Few people know this better than neurologist and president and board chairwoman of the Voluntary Anti-Doping Association, the venerated former ringside physician, Dr. Margaret Goodman.

"When someone is getting hit in the head for a living, [performance-enhancing drugs] certainly shouldn't be allowable."

I spoke with her at length about performance-enhancing drugs in contact sports, spending the better part of the conversation with mouth agape at both the ubiquity of enhancements and the unscrutinized danger they impose. But one only need look up chronic traumatic encephalopathy, or CTE, to spot this dirty little secret. Our conversation was rife with grim reminders of football players who, upon autopsy, were found to suffer from CTE, high schoolers and college athletes with concurrent, unhealed brain trauma, former NCAA [National Collegiate Athletic Association] football players instructed to fail their baseline concussion tests, to bolster the odds they'd get back in the game. Fold in anabolic steroids that, along with boosting muscle mass, artificially boost healing, and things start to look scary. Harder hits, and a shorter healing time for the body—but not necessarily the brain?

"When the smoke clears and they start really looking at the studies of who developed [CTE], as far as amateur and professional athletes, when [they] start getting larger numbers and start really looking at the risk factors, you are going to definitely see that PED use contributed."

Her voice is edged with determined frustration.

"When you amplify [the dangers of contact sports] via an athlete being on performance-enhancing drugs or using performance-enhancing methods, the risks become that much greater.

"To me, there's just no right or wrong in this."

The use of performance-enhancing drugs is an undoubtedly pervasive and complicated issue. This isn't the sole purvey of cycling; it's everywhere. From elite athletes to NCAA soccer players, athletes are slurping down, shooting up, and rubbing in untested, unstudied, risky, and potentially deadly cocktails of so-called enhancers. And there are no easy answers.

Doesn't Everybody Do It?

Like a metastatic tumor with tendrils snaked deep through the body, the issue of PEDs spreads in many different directions: autonomy, exploitation, money, psychology, desperation, and competition. It's big and it's messy and there are no easy answers or quick fixes. But it's also small, private, and personal. This isn't just theory. These are bodies: fragile bits of meat wrapped around bones responding to electrical impulses from a soft mass encased by a thick dome. It's easy to forget that bodies are sensitive, fussy things. They demand that their components fall within thousands of specific parameters. Temperature, pH, hormonal levels, blood glucose and micronutrients are just a few of the many areas where a body must stay within a certain range in order to stay alive. Athletes who have already pushed themselves to the limits of human performance, who would like to push further, can and do so with the help of a variety of drugs and a supportive environment. Trainers, friends, competitors, doctors, all at the ready to help in the pursuit of the win. Don't worry, everybody does it. Don't you want to win? Take this, you'll piss clean. Did you hear that the guy you're fighting is enhanced? So-and-so took this and got a full scholarship. You hear that what's his name is on that new shit? If it was dangerous, no one would do it. Don't worry. Don't worry. It's safe. Everybody does it. *It's only fair.*

It's a seductive world of limitless promise, but to buy into genetic determinism in sport, to use that as the basis of rationalizing risky, pharmacological glory, is a dangerous mistake.

And it makes Malcolm Gladwell an extraordinarily dangerous journalist.

Periodical and Internet Sources Bibliography

The following articles have been selected to supplement the diverse views presented in this chapter.

America	"Touching Ethical Bases," September 9, 2013.
BusinessWire	"Survey Reveals That Majority of Americans Believe Olympics Less Enjoyable Due to Doping," January 28, 2014.
CNN	"Performance Enhancing Drugs in Sports Fast Facts," August 6, 2014.
Mike Downey	"Baseball, This Time Throw the Book at Users of Performance-Enhancing Drugs," CNN, June 6, 2013.
David Ewing Duncan	"The Cyborg Olympic Games: If Performance Enhancements Were Legal," *Newsweek*, February 20, 2014.
Economist	"Doping in Sport: Athlete's Dilemma," July 20, 2013.
Nathan Fenno	"Penalties for PEDs Need to Be Draconian," *Washington Times*, July 24, 2013.
Tracee Hamilton	"Athletes and PEDs: The Accident Excuse Is Getting Hard to Swallow," *Washington Post*, February 25, 2013.
George J. Mitchell	"Drugs in Sports: An Ongoing Menace," *Washington Post*, January 14, 2014.
Ryan Purcell	"Performance Enhancement: To Embrace Doping in Sport Is Absurd," *Nature*, August 9, 2012.
Troy E. Renck	"PED Users in Major League Baseball Will Be Hit with Tougher Penalties," *Denver Post*, March 29, 2014.

OPPOSING
VIEWPOINTS®
SERIES

CHAPTER 2

How Dangerous Are Performance-Enhancing Drugs?

Chapter Preface

Not all performance-enhancing drugs (PEDs) in sports are to make athletes faster or stronger. Banned by the World Anti-Doping Agency (WADA), diuretics increase the body's production of urine. Sometimes called "water pills," there are three types of diuretics: thiazide, loop, and potassium-sparing. Athletes take them to meet weight requirements in a short time or mask the presence of other PEDs in their urine. "Over the years, the total number of occurrences has been increasing; this trend of increasing positive findings may be due not only to an increase in abuse, but is likely due to improved methods of detection," states researcher Amy B. Cadwallader and her colleagues in the *British Journal of Pharmacology*.

One recent case involving diuretics emerged in June 2013. Veronica Campbell-Brown, a Jamaican track-and-field athlete and seven-time Olympic medalist, tested positive for hydrochlorothiazide. However, after receiving a provisional suspension, Campbell-Brown was cleared of the charges in February 2014. The Jamaica Anti-Doping Commission allegedly did not follow the proper procedures in obtaining her urine sample. "If you can't guarantee the integrity of the sample, then nothing after that matters because you can't say that it's her urine or that the sample wasn't tampered with," maintains Howard Jacobs, Campbell-Brown's attorney.

Although viewed as generally safe, diuretics can have side effects if overused, ranging from uncomfortable to potentially serious conditions. "Diuretic medications can be dangerous to one's health, completely throwing off electrolyte balances," asserts physician Max S. Chartrand. "Most are prescribed based upon scant information and very little medical examination." Depending on the type of diuretics taken, users may develop too much or too little potassium in their blood, which can be life threatening. Other problems linked to diuretics include gout, impotence, and enlarged breasts in men.

Diuretics are just one example of drugs athletes may abuse to enhance their performance while incurring serious side effects and life-threatening conditions. In the following chapter, authors expand upon the dangers of performance-enhancing drugs and their effect on athletes and nonathletes alike.

| *"With so many grave risks, are the perceived benefits worth it?"*

Performance-Enhancing Drugs Are Dangerous

Chris Doorley

In the following viewpoint, Chris Doorley warns that athletes using performance-enhancing drugs (PEDs) risk their health and lives. He focuses on "the big three" prohibited by the World Anti-Doping Agency: synthetic testosterone, erythropoietin (EPO), and human growth hormone (HGH). Long-term use of lab-made testosterone, Doorley says, can result in liver abnormalities, cholesterol problems, and other severe repercussions. Another anabolic agent, HGH can impair heart function; lead to type 2 diabetes; and deteriorate joints, connective tissues, and muscles, he explains. EPO is linked to strokes, heart attacks, and lung blood clots, maintains Doorley, causing the deaths of many cyclists. Doorley is a writer and editor based in San Francisco, California.

As you read, consider the following questions:

1. What diseases can athletes contract when using synthetic testosterone, as stated by Doorley?

"Performance Enhancing Drugs and the Modern Olympian," from Inside NOVA website (http://www.pbs.org/wgbh/nova/insidenova/2012/07/ped.html) © 2012 WGBH Educational Foundation.

2. As described by Doorley, how does HGH weaken heart function?

3. What does the author purport about the competitive benefits of PEDs?

I'll be watching the Olympics again this year [in 2012] whenever I can. I'll watch for the explosive performances and tight finishes on the track and field. I'll look for the photo-finish touch in the pool. I'll be tuning in for gymnastics' superhuman-like shows of power and balance.

And, I'll be watching a new Olympic pastime: seeing who gets caught using performance-enhancing drugs, or PEDs. "Citius, Altius, Fortius"—the Olympic motto—translates to: Faster, Higher, Stronger. Does that sentiment drive some athletes to seek enhanced results?

This [viewpoint] marks the beginning of a blog series covering PEDs and how they have affected Olympic games and athletes. PEDs have profoundly changed modern sporting contests and media coverage of them for decades. In addition to the Major League Baseball steroid scandals and July's renewed accusations of Lance Armstrong's blood doping, there have been instances and investigations of doped Olympians dating back to East German and Soviet-era athletes more than 40 years ago.

Only more recently have governing bodies—namely the World Anti-Doping Agency, "WADA," which tests international contests such as London's 2012 Olympics—attempted to test for and regulate their use and abuse. Along with competitive advantages, PEDs carry severe health risks. They can even kill.

Dr. William Mitchell is an orthopedic surgeon and an expert on this subject, having worked with professional and amateur athletes in greater Boston for more than 25 years and having served as contributing editor to *The Encyclopedia of Sports Medicine*. Of the many drugs on the black market,

Mitchell spotlights "the big three": erythropoietin, or EPO; human growth hormone, also known as HGH; and synthetic testosterone. All are prominently featured on WADA's nine-page list of prohibited substances, which went into effect on January 1 this year. It provides the standard for prohibited chemicals among international athletes and will guide official Olympic testing in coming weeks.

Synthetic Testosterone—At the Top of the List

Dr. Mitchell walked me through the first section of WADA on anabolic agents, or synthetic versions of testosterone. At the top of the long list are the lab-made hormones androstenediol and androstenedione. Along with many similar anabolics, these are laboratory-made versions of the body's main strength-inducing hormone, testosterone.

Both men and women produce testosterone naturally. It imparts primary sex characteristics in males, like a deep voice, facial hair and sexual organs. In both genders, it metabolizes amino acids from the diet into the proteins that make up muscle fibers. Therefore, the more testosterone in the body, the more muscle-building potential.

Athletes take these synthetic forms of testosterone hoping to gain strength and muscle density, decrease recovery time after training, and reduce the incidence of injury during intense workouts.

But side effects of these drugs go beyond the simple risk of being caught using. Rage, depression, severe acne and baldness, in both genders, may be the best-known side effects. Less widely circulated are the more severe repercussions of chronic use, like liver abnormalities and tumors, heart and circulatory impairment, cholesterol risks, and the added danger of contracting infectious diseases, like HIV or hepatitis, from shared needles. Every one of these can be life threatening. Because of these dangers, and the use of anabolic agents across so many athletes in multiple sports, the WADA ranked them at the top of their prohibited list, said Mitchell.

Scrolling down the document, you don't have to go far to find the second and third of Mitchell's "big three," HGH and EPO.

HGH—Similar to Testosterone

Like the "andro-" drugs, HGH is an anabolic hormone very similar to testosterone. Naturally secreted by the pituitary gland in both sexes, it too increases muscle mass. Mitchell relates it very closely to testosterone in that HGH builds proteins from the food we eat so that bone and muscle can grow in density. Olympians in strength and speed events—sprinting, power lifting, swimming, boxing—may be competing against athletes who have used HGH.

Technically, HGH is available only by doctor's prescription, and it is typically used to help young children with deficiencies leading to inhibited growth. Though it hasn't been studied as a performance enhancer—the ethical implications of such a study are troubling—baseball fans allegedly saw it in action in Barry Bonds. HGH increased Bonds' muscle mass along with his shoe size and even his skull size, said Mitchell.

"That's human growth hormone," he said. "That's what it does."

HGH brings its own set of risks. Topping the list is cardiomyopathy, an enlarging and thickening of muscles in the heart, that weakens heart function over time. HGH can also impair glucose regulation, leading to type 2 diabetes. Over prolonged use, joints, tendons, ligaments and muscles can deteriorate, causing an ironic lack of strength in the aging HGH athlete.

EPO—A Cause of Bleeding Events

This brings us to the last of the "big three," EPO. The drug, epoetin alfa, is a laboratory version of erythropoietin, a natu-

Playing Russian Roulette with Health

Unfortunately, it's too early to determine the final outcome, in particular cases, but the fact of the matter is that in addition to whatever sport doping athletes may be playing, they have also started a game of Russian roulette with their health. They may end up being lucky and not having serious side effects, but they may not. Ask the parents of athletes who have died from "heart attacks" in their twenties whether they think that drug use had some impact on what happened. Ask the current sufferers of heart, liver, kidney and other disorders whether, if they could turn the clock back, they would still have used drugs to improve their sport performance. Ask the women in their twenties who are having trouble conceiving or whose children have fetal disorders what they think now about the drugs they took for sport, or the men who suffer from low sperm count and impotence if they still feel the invincibility of their youth. Would you give up the ability to have children for a momentary edge in some sport competition? Kids need to be protected from themselves if they do not have enough sense on their own. Parents, coaches and teachers, even friends, have to learn to watch for the signs. If drug use is stopped soon enough, many of the long-term effects may be eliminated or at least reduced.

Dick Pound, Inside Dope: How Drugs Are the Biggest Threat to Sports, Why You Should Care, and What Can Be Done About Them. *Mississauga, ON: J. Wiley & Sons Canada, 2006.*

rally occurring hormone produced by the kidneys and liver that stimulates red blood cell production by the bone marrow. By helping to increase the number of red blood cells, which contain hemoglobin molecules that transport oxygen from the blood to the muscle, EPO boosts the amount of fuel muscles have to burn for energy. In medical applications, it has been used to treat lack of blood iron, or anemia, in patients with greatly impaired kidney function from diseases like AIDS. It can also be used before surgery, like open-heart procedures, to counter the effects of anticipated blood loss.

But, it has been implicated in the death of at least 18 cyclists during alleged heavy use in the 1990s. These cyclists were victims of bleeding events: stroke, heart attack, and blood clots in the lungs called pulmonary edemas.

With so many grave risks, are the perceived benefits worth it? In fact, none of PEDs' touted performance benefits—taken at high doses acquired on the unregulated black market, and with prolonged use or abuse—have been proven. After all, giving athletes high doses of dangerous drugs for research purposes would be highly unethical.

Mitchell agrees: "Doping increases health risks when doses and amounts of hormonal use is not regulated and can lead to overdosing and catastrophic health risks including death."

"Some substances do cause health problems. But so might many sports."

The Dangers of Professional Sports Are Comparable to That of Performance-Enhancing Drugs

Michael Lavin

In the following viewpoint, Michael Lavin proposes that the risks involved in professional sports are similar to those of performance-enhancing drugs (PEDs). Lavin suggests that most forms of training—which enhance performance—elevate the risks athletes face. The author also argues that many sports are hazardous to health—boxing causes more brain damage than drugs, and playing football can cut players' lives short and disable them. However, the prohibition of PEDs, he reasons, does not consider the athlete's assumption of risk. Based in San Antonio, Texas, Lavin is a psychologist at the Brooke Army Medical Center's intensive outpatient program.

As you read, consider the following questions:

1. What is the high road to excellence in sports, in Lavin's view?

2. As claimed by the author, how do the public and athletes make the distinction between PEDs and non-performance-enhancing drugs?

3. In what ways can assuming a risk be rationalized, as described in the viewpoint?

Anybody watching sports with even casual attention can hit upon one truth fast. The race does not always belong to the fast and strong, but that is the way to bet. Parents teach children the tale of the tortoise and the hare, but not to let the young know what to expect when a tortoise and a hare race. Instead, it is a cautionary tale. Even somebody with a natural advantage can lose for want of effort and character. And if an industrious, tenacious hare can beat a loafing hare, imagine the advantage an industrious, tenacious hare has over the most conscientious of tortoises.

Hard Training Matters

Professional athletes understand that hard training matters. Flip through any issue of any magazine devoted to sports, especially issues with training tips. These articles spill over with evidence of a devotion to training as extreme as the Rules for the Order of [Saint] Benedict. The modern athlete is no casual amateur. To win in modern games, athletes pursue a way of life. Gone are Babe Ruth diets of beer and hot dogs. Modern athletes have dieticians, sports psychologists, physicians, physical trainers, and gangs of coaches to anneal them for the rigors of modern competitions. Lawyers are at the ready to protect other interests. Still, despite the pampering, athletes work hard. Anybody who reads of the training regimens of Michael Phelps, Lance Armstrong, the Williams sisters [Venus and Serena] must stand in awe of them. And gone are the days when baseball, basketball, or football players spent off seasons delivering beer or anchoring couches. They train.

With winning linked to maximizing coordination, strength, speed, and endurance, competitive athletes seek all the advantages they can, and they have the drug tests to prove it. The current (circa 2009) spate of stories on steroid use among major league players, including the confession of erstwhile-denier Alex Rodriguez, the game's premier player, and the indictment of Barry Bonds, baseball's premier sultan of swat and steadfast denier, is one example. The Olympics of 2008 had its drugs scandals as has had the Tour de France. One could move through the sports. Of course sports that put a premium on muscle have more steroid abuse than sports that do not. Distance runners prefer methods like blood doping to bulking up on steroids. The archer may prefer a beta blocker.

Two Roads to Excellence

The modern, money-fueled drive for athletic supremacy has morphed strength athletes into behemoths. Behold their wide bodies—compare the sizes of recent baseball, football, basketball, and tennis players—as athletes seek all advantages to win to players of fifty or even twenty years ago. As always, people have noticed two roads to excellence: the high road and the low road.

The touted road is the high road. It is supposedly, despite the extraordinary evolution of modern training, based on old, laudable traditions. It is part of the general culture. Athletes unhesitatingly acknowledge hard work in the gym, natural talent or, for the religiously preoccupied, God-given talent, hours of practice, eating right, staying away from bad food and influences, wonderful teammates, superb coaches, their loving parents, devoted spouse, their faith in sports-approving God, overcoming addiction to booze or other chemical temptresses, doctors who rehabilitated injured joints as indispensable contributors, generally in a crowd-pleasing combination. These ingredients pave the high road.

Athletes tend to deny any travel on the low road until either out of competition or compelled by an avalanche of evidence to confess. They do not stand on the podium and proclaim that anabolic steroids or other miracles of chemistry have been the *sine qua non* [an essential element or condition] of their wins. They no more like to admit this than coaches do that stealing their opponent's playbook made winning much easier than it might otherwise have been. The low road is paved with low means.

The Distinction Between Performance- and Non-Performance-Enhancing Drugs

Over 20 years ago, I addressed this topic. At that time, as now, it was common to accept dubious distinctions regarding drugs. For example, even now, otherwise astute commentators continue to embrace a distinction between performance- and non-performance-enhancing drugs. A typical example of a performance enhancer is an anabolic steroid, a drug that is believed to enhance an athlete's ability to train hard, build muscle, and recover fast to train still more. An analgesic would count as a non-performance-enhancing drug. To think about this for a second is to encounter problems. Consider an arthritic, asthmatic older man. Let's call him "Mike." With his medications, Mike can train in Aikido [a martial art]. Without his medications, he has difficulty training for more than 15 minutes. There is almost a fourfold gain when Mike takes Advair, Tylenol, or, in extreme cases, Indocin or Albuterol to manage his asthma and arthritis. Likewise, depressive athletes may fail to train at all unless they take their Prozac. Likewise, athletes reinjecting their own blood is banned, though one must contort words to count blood as a drug. The World Anti-Doping Agency (WADA) publishes a list of proscribed drugs that is striated with drugs from all kinds of pharmaceutical categories. And, in fact, some WADA proscribed drugs, beta blockers for one, are only banned for some sports.

In practice, the distinction between performance-enhancing drugs (PEDs) and non-performance-enhancing drugs does not arise from the lay public or athletes having a grasp of pharmacology that enables them to know what counts as a PED. Instead, they are taught. They grow up in a community that distinguishes licit and illicit means to wins and records. In virtue of growing up in this community, athletes and the public learn to make relevant distinctions. Over time, lawyers and the like get involved. Lists of banned substances evolve as well as policing policies. Anabolic steroids make the list, but aspirin does not. The means to high athletic achievement are purportedly limited to the high road, which itself is evolving. As anybody with eyes can tell, the current high road calls for more weight training than it did 50 years ago. Gone are the halcyon days when champagne-swigging aristocrats set aside their bubbling flutes to show how well they can sprint and hurdle as in *Chariots of Fire*. Today's athletes are no amateurs. Instead, they have succumbed to a ruthless professionalism that has commodified sport and turned gifted and popular athletes into corporations.

The Criteria Fail

If anybody has doubts about how feeble attempts to identify a defensible set of conditions that segregate PEDs from other drugs, foods, or even training methods, consider the World Anti-Doping Agency's code.

The relevant section runs as follows:

> 'A substance shall be considered for inclusion on the Prohibited List if the substance is a masking agent or meets two of the following three criteria: (1) it has the potential to enhance or enhances sport performance; (2) it represents a potential or actual health risk; or (3) it is contrary to the spirit of sport.'

Health May Not Be a Primary Basis for Drug Bans

From what has been said, it is clear that while there may indeed be potentially dangerous side effects associated with the use of certain banned drugs, much the same may also be said about many drugs which are not banned and which are widely used within the sporting context. . . . Obvious examples include caffeine and ephedrine, the latter being readily available to the public in over-the-counter cold remedies. These inconsistencies—and in particular the fact that several potentially dangerous drugs are used perfectly legally within sport—suggest that, whatever the ideological rhetoric linking sport and health, considerations of health may not constitute the primary basis underlying the decision to ban certain drugs but not others.

Ivan Waddington, Sport, Health and Drugs:
A Critical Sociological Perspective.
New York: E & FN Spon, 2000, pp. 104–105.

However to this the new code now adds further justification clearly aimed at rebutting the criticisms of the earlier version:

> 'None of the three criteria alone is a sufficient basis for adding a substance to the Prohibited List. Using the potential to enhance performance as the sole criteria would include, for example, physical and mental training, red meat, carbohydrate loading and training at altitude. Risk of harm would include smoking. Requiring all three criteria would also be unsatisfactory. For example, the use of genetic transfer technology to dramatically enhance

sport performance should be prohibited as contrary to the spirit of sport even if it is not harmful. Similarly, the potentially unhealthy abuse of certain substances without therapeutic justification based on the mistaken belief they enhance performance is certainly contrary to the spirit of sport regardless of whether the expectation of performance enhancement'.

The criteria as stated fail. Most training that enhances athletic performance elevates risk. For example, practicing hockey and gymnastics is dangerous and enhances performance. Likewise, analgesics and organ meat may enhance performance and carry risks, but nobody is pressing to outlaw either aspirin or liver. The WADA authors leave it a mystery, and a dark one at that, as to why only certain risky, performance-enhancing substances and methods make its list and not others. The spirit of sport, whatever it be, seems to drive the list.

An Athlete's Assumption of Risk

What's more, WADA fails to consider what rationalizes an athlete's assumption of a risk. One reason for training long and hard, for sacrificing an ordinary life, is that for victorious athletes the potential rewards are enormous.

Almost a century ago, [H.T.] Terry delineated the rationality of assuming a risk. In particular, how probable are the harms of a risky act? How grave are these harms? How probable is it that enduring the harms will achieve the goals for which they were assumed? How valuable are these goals? How necessary is the risk to achieve the goals? If WADA authors took account of these notions in constructing their lists, the account is invisible. After all, given the world as it is, the Michael Phelpses of the world do rather better than archers or Judo champions in turning gold medals into big money. If so, analyses of risk like Terry's have as a consequence that athletes have better reasons for taking risks in some sports than in others.

Despite the deficiencies of what the WADA authors wrote, their effort does offer guidance and processes for protecting athletes from unjust accusations. Further, the WADA authors did the service of stating what values it believes are tied to the "spirit of sport." As the WADA authors put it:

> The spirit of sport is the celebration of the human spirit, body and mind, and is characterized by the following values:
>
> - Ethics, fair play and honesty
> - Health
> - Excellence in performance
> - Character and education
> - Fun and joy
> - Teamwork
> - Dedication and commitment
> - Respect for rules and laws
> - Respect for self and other participants
> - Courage
> - Community and solidarity
>
> Doping is fundamentally contrary to the spirit of sport.

What is confusing is how one moves from these values to judgments that particular drugs are contrary to the spirit of sport. There is also an implicit tension regarding the type of justification being offered. This confusion pervades every man thinking about drugs in sport. Do the values justify prohibitions, or do they show substance use is wrong, if there are prohibitions? . . .

Some substances do cause health problems. But so might many sports. Boxing many abbreviate a boxer's years of clear thinking far faster than any drug. Football may abbreviate the lives of athletes or leave them crippled. Old training practices like refusing athletes water do not violate the rules of sport, but seem to kill boys every year or so. Further, as the earlier discussion of Terry on risk shows, the level of rationally defensible risk varies with a number of other factors, including expected gains.

| "Athletes still use these substances today, and they have been joined by nonathletes—some of whom simply want to look good."

Performance-Enhancing Drugs Are Dangerous to Nonathletes

Marifel Mitzi F. Fernandez and Robert G. Hosey

Seeking an edge, nonathletes use an array of performance-enhancing drugs (PEDs), state Marifel Mitzi F. Fernandez and Robert G. Hosey in the following viewpoint. Recreational bodybuilders who want to improve their appearance, they explain, may unknowingly take a "natural" supplement with harmful side effects, while others obtain illegal steroids. Going by many names, the types of PEDs taken by nonathletes range from agents such as human growth hormone (HGH) and other drugs to build muscle and strength to unexpected substances such as caffeine and Viagra to improve athletic performance, maintain the authors. Based in Saint Paul, Minnesota, Fernandez is a physician specializing in sports medicine. Hosey is a physician and professor of family and community medicine at the University of Kentucky.

Marifel Mitzi F. Fernandez and Robert G. Hosey, "Performance-Enhancing Drugs Snare Nonathletes, Too," *Journal of Family Practice* , vol. 58, January 2009, pp. 16–18, 20–22.

As you read, consider the following questions:

1. According to Fernandez and Hosey, why do users of anabolic androgenic steroids (AAS) not tell their physicians of their activities?

2. What are the side effects of ephedrine, as stated by the authors?

3. As warned by Fernandez and Hosey, when can caffeine cause serious cardiovascular effects and death?

JC, a 23-year-old man, is in your office for evaluation of high blood pressure, after failing a commercial driver's license exam the previous week. He has been your patient for the past 10 years, and his previous annual physicals have been unremarkable. He is 5'10" tall, weighs 209 pounds, and has a muscular build. His blood pressure today is 160/90 and his heart rate is 62 and regular. The rest of his physical exam is normal.

He is a nonsmoker, rarely uses alcohol, and denies illicit drug use. He exercises regularly, has been taking some protein shakes and what he refers to as a "natural" supplement. His lab work shows some elevation in his aspartate aminotransferase (AST) and alanine aminotransferase (ALT), with a negative hepatitis panel. The rest of his metabolic panel is within normal limits.

JC was on the track team in high school, and since graduation has continued to work out and stay fit. You ask him if he takes steroids, and he tells you he was warned about the risks of anabolic androgenic steroids (AAS) in high school. He sticks to a "natural" supplement, which he buys online or through friends at the gym. Still, you know that elevated liver enzymes and hypertension can be associated with AAS use and that dietary supplements don't have to meet the same standards the Food and Drug Administration (FDA) imposes on drugs. You warn him that supplements aren't always safe, and ask him to bring in his supplement bottle so you can go over the label and, possibly, have the contents tested.

Pursuit of That "Edge" Extends Beyond Olympians

Even before the start of the modern Olympic games, athletes have used ergogenic aids—substances used to enhance performance, energy, or work capacity—to give themselves a "competitive edge." Athletes still use these substances today, and they have been joined by nonathletes—some of whom simply want to look good.

A 2004 Internet study of AAS users reported that the majority are recreational bodybuilders or nonathletes. Twenty-five percent of participants in this survey reported starting using steroids during their teenage years.

An ongoing study of high school students and young adults indicates an AAS use prevalence rate of 1.1% to 2.3% in boys and 0.4% to 0.6% in girls. Approximately 40% of survey participants noted that obtaining steroids was relatively easy.

The Centers for Disease Control and Prevention (CDC) reports that 4.4% to 5.7% of boys (grades 9 through 12) have used illegal steroids and that 1.9% to 3.8% of girls have.

Few AAS users tell their physicians of their steroid use. Part of the reason, of course, is that illegal substance use is stigmatized and can lead to prosecution. Another reason, though, is that these patients think physicians don't know much about these substances. Still other patients, like JC, don't tell because they may not even be aware that some substances billed as "natural" conceal potential dangers. . . .

Performance-Enhancing Drugs Go by Many Names

Refining your care of patients who are taking performance-enhancing drugs requires that you know the various names these drugs go by, the reason your patients may be taking them, and the adverse effects associated with them. This review . . . will help.

Anabolic androgenic steroids: Often paired with energy drinks

Teenagers may refer to AAS as "pumpers," "gym candy," or "juice." Trade names for AAS are Dianabol, Anadrol, Deca Durabolin, Parabolin, and Winstrol. AAS are often used with nutritional supplements like creatine, multivitamins, and energy drinks, in the belief that these regimens will make the user stronger, more muscular, and a better athlete.

AAS are synthetic analogues of testosterone and come in oral, injectable, and transdermal forms. At supraphysiologic doses, testosterone has been found to increase lean body (fat-free) mass and muscle strength in humans. The anabolic effects are more pronounced when AAS are used at higher doses over longer periods of time, especially when combined with a strength-training program. AAS have also been found to stimulate the production of growth hormone and insulin-like growth factor and to counteract the catabolic effects of cortisol.

The use and possession of AAS without a doctor's prescription is illegal in the United States. A majority of AAS users buy their medications through Internet suppliers, with some of the drugs being manufactured overseas or in illicit labs. Substandard quality control in manufacture poses an increased health risk to consumers.

Adverse effects include injection site pain, acne, baldness, gynecomastia, testicular atrophy, sexual dysfunction, and psychological disturbances (also known as "roid rage"). Increases in liver enzymes with the oral forms of AAS have also been noted. In the prepubertal athlete, premature physeal closure may occur, resulting in permanent short stature. Women who take AAS may have virilization effects, menstrual irregularities, and early menopause.

The cardiovascular risks of AAS use are substantial. High-dose and long-term AAS use has been linked to cardiomyopathy and sudden death. Some data suggest the development of accelerated atherosclerosis with AAS use, leading to hypertension, coronary artery disease (CAD), and acute myocardial infarction. An unfavorable lipid panel has also been noted, with an increase in LDL [low-density lipoprotein] and decreased HDL [high-density lipoprotein].

Tetrahydrogestrinone: A "designer" steroid

Tetrahydrogestrinone (THG) was initially developed to avoid detection by testing protocols current at the time. This drug has garnered significant media attention in the past few years because of scandals involving professional and Olympic athletes. THG is chemically related to 2 other banned steroids, trenbolone and gestrinone. It is used similarly to AAS to increase muscle bulk and enhance performance. It is more hepatotoxic than AAS, with highly potent androgenic and progestin properties in in vitro bioassay studies.

Marketing of this agent is banned in the United States. There are no long-term studies of its effectiveness or side effect profile.

Androstenedione: Initially an anti-aging drug

Androstenedione, aka Andromax and Androstat 100, is a precursor of testosterone. This substance is produced in the adrenal glands and gonads. Initially marketed as a dietary supplement and anti-aging drug, it was banned by the FDA in 2004 because of its potent anabolic and androgenic effects. Ergogenic use includes promoting muscle building and strength and fat reduction. Studies on healthy young men found no improvement in skeletal muscle adaptation to resistance training with androstenedione supplementation for 8 to 12 weeks. Studies of its effect on increasing blood testosterone levels are conflicting. Several studies noted an increase in estradiol levels after oral androstenedione supplementation.

Endocrine pathways with this drug are similar to AAS, and the side effect profile is similar as well, although not as pronounced. Larger, long-term studies are needed to fill out this drug's profile and document its effects on the athletes who use it.

Dehydroepiandrosterone: Marketed as a "wonder drug"

Dehydroepiandrosterone (DHEA), marketed under the names Prastera, Fidelin, and Fluasterone, is another precursor of testosterone. It is produced in the adrenal cortex and has weak androgenic properties. DHEA is a dietary supplement marketed as a "wonder drug" and, like androstenedione, is advertised to promote muscle building and fat burning. It is also said to have anti-aging properties. DHEA has been used by athletes in the belief that it will increase testosterone levels and muscle bulk.

In studies done in healthy men, however, even large doses of DHEA (1600 mg/d) did not result in an increase in testosterone levels. An increase in estradiol levels was noted in elderly men. Women who supplement with DHEA were found to have increased levels of testosterone and virilization effects, even at small doses (25–50 mg/d). Because of the risk of these side effects and the lack of long-term studies, DHEA supplementation is not recommended for use by adolescents or women. There is no convincing evidence to support claims of the anabolic and anti-aging effects of DHEA.

Human growth hormone: Side effects include hypertension

Human growth hormone (HGH) is an endogenous pituitary hormone with anabolic functions that increases muscle mass without the androgenic side effects. It is used medically for patients with decreased endogenous levels of GH or dwarfism. As an ergogenic aid, it has been found to increase levels of insulin-like growth factors, and the combination leads to increased protein synthesis and muscle mass.

Side effects of HGH include insulin resistance, GH-induced myopathy, and acromegaly-like effects. There have been re-

85

ports of hypertension, cardiomegaly, ventricular hypertrophy, and abnormal lipids with excessive use. Premature physeal closure may occur in the adolescent HGH user. It's unclear whether HGH actually enhances sports performance, because the evidence is insufficient.

Ephedrine: Used by hockey players

Ephedrine is a stimulant derived from the herb *ma huang*. It goes by many names, among them Ma Huang, Bolt ephedrine, Asia Black 25, Hot Body Ephedra, and Thin Quik. Its chemical structure is related to amphetamine. Among college athletes, ephedrine and amphetamine use is more common in power sports, those requiring increased concentration (e.g., rifle shooting, fencing), ice hockey, and field sports. Users feel less fatigue, experience bursts of energy, and lose weight.

Users may experience irritability, anxiety, insomnia, and tremors, especially if stimulants are used in conjunction with high doses of caffeine. Ephedrine stimulates the release of norepinephrine, which produces increases in blood pressure, peripheral vascular resistance, and heart rate. These norepinephrine effects are the proposed mechanism for reported cases of myocardial infarction, cerebral artery vasoconstriction, and stroke associated with ephedrine use.

Marketing of dietary supplements that contain ephedrine has been banned by the FDA because of the stimulant's potential for increasing cardiovascular and stroke risks.

Caffeine: May give sprinters a leg up

Caffeine—which is found in everything from coffee to energy tablets and energy drinks—increases a person's energy level. In endurance sports, it also increases time to exhaustion. Studies in endurance-trained cyclists have shown that caffeine intake reduced leg pain, increased maximal leg force, and lengthened time to fatigue. A recent study in Australia also showed that caffeine may improve intermittent-sprint performance in competitive male athletes.

Serious cardiovascular risks and even death have been documented when caffeine has been used with other stimulants, such as ephedrine or amphetamines. The combination of high doses of caffeine and ephedrine has a potential for life-threatening arrhythmia, hypertension, and stroke. Other psychomotor side effects include anxiety, irritability, tremor, and the potential for withdrawal symptoms. Because of caffeine's stimulant nature, the International Olympic Committee and the National Collegiate Athletic Association have set urinary thresholds for its use in competition.

Erythropoietin: Promotes endurance

Erythropoietin (EPO) is a hormone produced in the kidneys that stimulates production of red blood cells (erythropoiesis). Marketed under the brand names Epogen and Procrit, EPO has legitimate medical uses. As an ergogenic substance, EPO is used to promote endurance by increasing the oxygen-carrying capacity of the blood with the increased red blood cell mass. In endurance athletes, the benefits of recombinant erythropoietin (rEpo) may last several weeks. There is also a practice called "blood doping," which is a transfusion prior to competition, to produce the same effect.

Adverse effects of EPO use are attributed to increased blood viscosity and thrombotic potential. Pulmonary embolism, stroke, myocardial infarction, and sudden death can occur. Cases of death due to severe bradycardia, usually occurring during the night, have also been reported. Development of anti-EPO antibodies may also occur, causing paradoxical anemia. Athletes found to be using rEpo are banned from competition by sports-governing organizations.

Creatine: Popular among body builders

Creatine is a popular supplement used by athletes and recreational bodybuilders to provide energy to skeletal muscles in short-duration, maximal exercise. It is an endogenous substance found mainly in skeletal muscle and is synthesized by the liver from the amino acids glycine, arginine, and methionine. It is also found in meat.

Creatine monohydrate supplements have been found to increase creatine stores in muscles. In the phosphorylated form, creatine serves as a substrate for adenosine triphosphate resynthesis during intense anaerobic exercise. Numerous studies support its ergogenic effect on short-term, intermittent maximal activities such as bodybuilding, swimming, and jumping. Similar benefits have not been proven for endurance aerobic activities, such as long-distance cycling or running.

This supplement is sold in many forms under such names as Rejuvenix, Cell-Tech Hardcore, Muscle Marketing, Femme Advantage, and NOS. Although not recommended for those under age 18, creatine is actually used by approximately 5.6% of high school athletes, with the highest levels of use (44%) occurring in the 11th and 12th grades. Reported side effects of creatine include muscle cramps, weight gain, and some minor gastrointestinal upset. Long-term studies on creatine supplementation are still needed.

Viagra (that's right, Viagra)

Viagra (sildenafil) is the latest entry in the list of drugs competitive athletes may be using to try to improve sports performance. The World Anti-Doping Agency is financing a study investigating whether sildenafil can create an unfair competitive advantage by dilating blood vessels and increasing oxygen-carrying capacity. Studies of the impact of sildenafil on exercise capacity of climbers at the Mt. Everest base camp and on exercise performance during acute hypoxia have been published. Sildenafil was found to improve athletic capacity in both. To date, no action has been taken to ban the substance in athletic competition.

Are Your Patients Using These Agents? Ask Them

Family physicians need to be alert to the red flags that may indicate steroid use and gently explore the full list of medications, over-the-counter products, and dietary supplements patients may be using. Take advantage of annual checkups and sports physicals to ask about use of performance-enhancing substances, educate patients on the risks involved, and emphasize good nutrition and sensible exercise routines as healthy ways to build a strong, attractive physique.

Education was certainly in order for your patient, JC, described at the beginning of this article. He thought the dietary supplement he used was natural and therefore harmless. Not so. It contained potentially dangerous substances, so you advised him to stop using it. Nutritional counseling and a vigorous exercise routine have allowed JC to maintain his fitness ideal. His blood pressure and liver enzymes returned to normal levels, and he passed his commercial driver's license exam.

> "Nine percent of teen girls reported try-
> ing synthetic HGH and 12 percent of
> boys."

Survey Finds Sharp Increase in Teen HGH Use

David Crary

In the following viewpoint, David Crary writes that the use of human growth hormone (HGH) has increased for teenagers. Teens are seduced by HGH, according to Crary, due to their desire to look better and perform better physically. The drug is dangerous, Crary states, and largely unregulated. The author writes that it is possible that teens are purchasing fake products and do not know what they are ingesting. In addition, he reports that the Mayo Clinic lists a number of side effects and hazards associated with HGH. Regardless of these issues, the author states, teens are ignoring the risks and continuing to use HGH.

As you read, consider the following questions:

1. According to the author, why is Travis Tygart not surprised by the increasing use of synthetic HGH among high school students?

2. In Crary's opinion, what attracts teens to HGH use?

3. What are some possible side effects, according to the Mayo Clinic?

Experimentation with human growth hormones by America's teens more than doubled in the past year, as more young people looked to drugs to boost their athletic performance and improve their looks, according to a new, large-scale national survey.

In a confidential 2013 survey of 3,705 high school students, being released Wednesday by the Partnership for Drug-Free Kids, 11 percent reported using synthetic HGH at least once—up from about 5 percent in the four preceding annual surveys. Teen use of steroids increased from 5 percent to 7 percent over the same period, the survey found.

Travis Tygart, CEO of the U.S. Anti-Doping Agency, depicted the numbers as alarming but not surprising, given the extensive online marketing of performance-enhancing substances and near-total lack of any drug testing for high school athletes.

"It's what you get when you combine aggressive promotion from for-profit companies with a vulnerable target—kids who want a quick fix and don't care about health risk," Tygart said in an interview. "It's a very easy sell, unfortunately."

Nine percent of teen girls reported trying synthetic HGH and 12 percent of boys.

"A picture emerges of teens—both boys and girls—entering a largely unregulated marketplace (online and in-store) in which performance-enhancing substances of many varieties are aggressively promoted with promises of improved muscle mass, performance and appearance," said the report. "This is an area of apparently growing interest and potential danger to teens that cries out for stricter controls on manufacture and marketing."

Given the high cost of authentic HGH, it's possible that some of the teens who reported using it may in fact have obtained fake products. As the survey said, "It's very difficult to know what exactly is in the substances teens are consuming, or what the short- and long-term impact on their health may be."

Steve Pasierb, president of the Partnership for Drug-Free Kids, said the motives of today's youthful dopers were different from the rebellious or escapist attitudes that traditionally accompanied teen drinking and pot smoking.

"This is about how you feel, how you look," Pasierb said. "They're doing this thing to get ahead. . . . Girls want to be thin and toned. For a lot of boys, it's about their six-pack."

He urged parents to talk candidly with their children about the dangers of performance-enhancing substances, but to avoid moralizing.

"It's not about illegality, or whether you're a good parent or bad parent," he said. "It's a health issue. These substances literally alter your body."

Pasierb said high school coaches have a key role in combatting doping. Some are vigilant, others oblivious and perhaps a third are prepared to tolerate doping in the interests of winning, he said.

The new survey noted that the upsurge in teen HGH use occurred even as famous athletes were caught up in high-profile doping cases. Last August, Major League Baseball punished Alex Rodriguez with a lengthy suspension after investigating his use of performance-enhancing drugs. A few months earlier, Lance Armstrong admitted in a TV interview to doping throughout his cycling career.

One of Armstrong's former teammates is Tyler Hamilton, who was forced to return his 2004 Olympic gold medal after being found guilty of doping. In recent public appearances, Hamilton has implored young athletes to resist the temptation to dope.

A Wide Range of Risks

A wide range of athletes, including weight lifters, baseball players, cyclists, and track-and-field participants, use HGH (human growth hormone) to build lean tissue and improve athletic performance. They inject HGH, believing that, because it isn't a steroid itself, it will provide the muscle gains they seek without the substantial risks of anabolic steroids. However, taken in large quantities, HGH causes the disease acromegaly, in which the body becomes huge and the organs and bones enlarge. Other risks of HGH include diabetes, thyroid disorder, heart disease, menstrual irregularities, diminished sexual desire, and shortened life span.

Frances Sizer and Ellie Whitney,
Nutrition: Concepts and Controversies. *13th edition.*
Belmont, CA: Wadsworth, Cengage Learning, 2013.

"There's so much pressure on winning—it's tough for these kids to stay true to themselves," he said. "I can't change every kid's mind, but if I can do my part and other people do their part, we can beat this monster."

Tygart, who as USADA's chief oversaw investigations of Armstrong and Hamilton, noted that stringent testing regimens are an increasingly effective deterrent to doping among athletes in major pro sports and in international competitions.

"But most young athletes are not in any testing program, and their chance of getting caught is zero," he said. "When left unchecked, the win-at-all-cost culture will take over and athletes will make the wrong decision."

Synthetic HGH is supposed to be available only by prescription, yet products claiming to contain HGH are widely promoted and enforcement of the regulations is inconsistent, Tygart said.

Among the groups seeking to reverse the teen doping trend is the Texas-based Taylor Hooton Foundation, named after a 17-year-old high school athlete whose suicide in 2003 was blamed by his family on his use of anabolic steroids. Its staff has spoken to thousands of young people at school assemblies and sports camps.

Donald Hooton Sr., Taylor's father and the foundation's president, depicted teen doping as an epidemic fueled by widespread ignorance among parents and coaches. He estimated that more than 1.5 million youths in the U.S. have tried steroids.

Information about teen use of performance-enhancing drugs is readily available online. The Mayo Clinic, for example, provides a list of possible hazards and side effects, including stunted growth, acne, liver problems, shrunken testicles for boys and excess facial hair for girls.

The clinic urges parents to check the ingredients of over-the-counter products used by their teens, and to be on the lookout for warning signs, including increased aggressiveness, rapid weight gain, and needle marks in the buttocks or thighs.

The Partnership for Drug-Free Kids survey also reported on other forms of substance abuse. Among its findings:

> Forty-four percent of teens report using marijuana at least once within their lifetime; 24 percent report using within the past month; and 7 percent report using at least 20 times within the past month. These levels have remained stable over the past five years.

After a sharp increase in teen misuse and abuse of prescription drugs in 2012, the rate remained stable in 2013, with 23 percent of teens reporting such abuse or misuse at least once. Fifteen percent reported having used the prescription painkillers Vicodin or OxyContin without a prescription at some point.

The survey of 3,705 students in grades 9–12 was conducted at their schools between February and June of 2013.

The margin of error was calculated at plus or minus 2.1 percentage points.

Founded in 1987, the New York–based Partnership for Drug-Free Kids is a nonprofit working to reduce teen substance abuse and support families affected by addiction.

> "One seldom-discussed feature about [human growth hormone] is that, despite the hoopla, it isn't really that dangerous."

Is HGH, Allegedly Alex Rodriguez's Drug of Choice, Really So Bad?

Kent Sepkowitz

Based in New York City, Kent Sepkowitz is an infectious-disease specialist and has written for the New York Times, Slate, *and* O, the Oprah Magazine. *In the following viewpoint, he asserts that the side effects of human growth hormone (HGH) are overblown compared to the dangers of anabolic steroids. HGH causes fatigue, fluid retention, and uncomfortable conditions such as carpal tunnel syndrome, Sepkowitz contends, while steroids heighten the risk of heart attack, stroke, and other serious illnesses, in addition to driving users to "roid rage." Furthermore, team owners show little concern for the overall health of players, who are pushed to play through injuries, he maintains.*

As you read, consider the following questions:

1. How do steroids and HGH differ as hormones, according to the author?

2. What is unknown about HGH administered to athletes at Biogenesis, as stated by the author?

3. What does the author recommend to hold team owners accountable for players' use of performance-enhancing drugs (PEDs)?

It appears that Major League Baseball is just about ready to give New York Yankees star Alex Rodriguez the boot, possibly for life. Although everything is at the rumor-only stage, accusations persist that A-Rod used human growth hormone [HGH], a performance-enhancing drug [PED], obtained from the Biogenesis [of America] enterprise formerly headquartered in Coral Gables, Fla. [He was suspended from the 2014 regular and post-season games.]

Setting aside whether Rodriguez is guilty or innocent, it's fair to ask where all the excitement about HGH comes from, as well as where, in the cosmology of illegal performance-enhancing substances, it sits. First of all, HGH is not a steroid, though the term "steroid" has come to be used interchangeably and incorrectly with PEDs. Steroids and HGH are both hormones—in this one aspect there is a similarity—but steroids are produced by the body to promote sexual differentiation, while HGH is involved in growth and maturation. Male hormones, androgens such as testosterone, make a guy a guy, horny and pimply and restless—and muscular. Jumping higher and running faster are possible as well. It clearly enhances performance, as the beneficiaries of baseball's last PED scandal, related to the Bay Area Laboratory Co-Operative, realized. But not only do anabolic steroids increase athletic performance, they also increase a person's risk of stroke, heart attack, and any number of bad-news illnesses. Stopping their use was a must.

A Relatively Sedate Hormone

Compared to 'roids, HGH is a relatively sedate amino acid, something people produce throughout life. Its effects are dramatic when levels are way too high or way too low. A common cause of dwarfism is an inadequate production of HGH. Its medical availability has made the diagnosis rare in countries with resources to diagnose and treat—the cost can run in the thousands of dollars per month. Others who, because of a tumor in the pituitary gland, may overproduce HGH develop a different problem: gigantism. Called acromegaly in medical parlance, it produces tall, gangly people ready for the basketball court, with thick jawbones and too-wide foreheads, as well as teeth that begin to spread apart as the lower jaw spreads. (Be on the lookout for older athletes with braces on their lower teeth.) A list of notable people who may have had acromegaly includes Lurch from *The Addams Family*, André the Giant, Jaws from the [James] Bond movie *The Spy Who Loved Me*, and perhaps Abraham Lincoln.

No Benefit for Athletic Performance

HGH until recently had an enormous advantage over steroids—it could not be detected. Now, with science moving ever forward and professional sports collective bargaining agreements accepting the need, HGH can be detected. But HGH is peculiar among PEDs in that, similar to deer antler spray, there is no evidence it helps athletic performance. The often-cited study looking at the effect of growth hormone on athletic performance was published in 2008 in the prestigious *Annals of Internal Medicine*. The authors pulled together the world's literature up to that point—27 studies comprising 303 persons, mostly healthy young men, who received HGH—and reviewed the results. Researchers had measured biceps and quadriceps, strength and endurance, body mass index, exercise capacity measured by speed and power, and indicators from blood samples of energy metabolism.

The studies found exactly no benefit, not even a tiny little one. Yes, it makes a fellah look the part, with bigger muscles and less fat, but if anything, HGH makes a guy feel more tired and leads to fluid retention in the face, hands, and ankles. In addition, it can lead to uncomfortable conditions such as carpal tunnel syndrome and other aches and pains. So why the rush to take an illegal substance that can make you look marvelous but does nothing for your home-run swing—and can lead to your eventual dismissal from the game you play so well? Are athletes really that dim?

The Unknowns of Biogenesis

Well, that's where the limits of the 2008 study start to show. We have no clue about three basic and important features of the alleged Biogenesis drug trafficking: how big and how frequent a dose the athletes were taking and for how long. The young male volunteers in the medical reports mentioned in the study took relatively tame doses for a relatively brief period. By contrast, if the accusations are true, A-Rod and the others involved with Biogenesis have been taking the drug for years, and at doses unknown to anyone—except perhaps Anthony Bosch, former proprietor of Biogenesis, whose feckless denials are classics of the form. It is likely that at the doses and frequency of administration that the pros use, there is a meaningful benefit.

One seldom-discussed feature about HGH is that, despite the hoopla, it isn't really that dangerous. Unlike steroids, which make a guy crazy, HGH is mostly a quality-of-life downer. It can deform a face, rarely cause diabetes, and make a person uncomfortable, but it doesn't push anyone over the edge in a 'roid rage, it doesn't shrivel the testicles, it doesn't make a person more annoying than the horniest frat guy you've ever been around.

Hold Team Owners Accountable

So why is Major League Baseball apparently so determined to throw the book at A-Rod and the rest of the Biogeniacs for a maybe-effective drug with troublesome but not life-threatening side effects? Surely it is not that they really are worried about the health of their employees. Players routinely are pushed and pulled, kneaded and given cortisone shots to get that sprained shoulder ready. Anything for the next big game— we'll worry about crippling arthritis and joint replacement and all the rest some other decade.

And it's hard to believe that commissioner and former owner Bud Selig, and Fred Wilpon and Little Steinbrenner and all the other team owners, are of such high ethical standards that the mere hint of impropriety is enough to cause conniptions and suspensions. I suspect that they enjoy the easy breeze of the sanctimonious common good. But if that indeed is their goal, then I have a very immodest suggestion: extend the ban to the owners. Just as a family who serves alcohol to someone who crashes a car while subsequently driving under the influence is liable for the accident, so too should the owners be tossed or fined when one of their employees is caught cheating. To fix the problem, it will never be enough to simply slap down the guy caught cheating, no matter how despicable he might be. Rather—to use a corporate boardroom language they all know so well—the boss too must be held accountable for his employees' actions. Any other approach is sure to whiff.

Periodical and Internet Sources Bibliography

The following articles have been selected to supplement the diverse views presented in this chapter.

Shawnee Barton	"In Defense of Human Growth Hormone," *Atlantic*, August 15, 2013.
Trevor Butterworth	"Don't Juice," *Newsweek*, July 9, 2012.
CNN	"Performance-Enhancing Drugs: Know the Risks," December 12, 2012.
Jonny Cooper	"Steroids: Supersizing the Man in the Mirror," *Telegraph*, May 1, 2014.
Diana Gonzalez	"Performance-Enhancing Drugs Becoming More Popular Among Non-Athletes," NBC 6 South Florida, August 8, 2013.
Health & Medicine Week	"New Poll: Young People Using Steroids and HGH Reaching Epidemic Status," October 25, 2013.
Elizabeth Foy Larsen	"Dangerously Strong: Anabolic Steroids Are Deadly—and Illegal. One Teen's Story Shows How the Pressure for Bigger Muscles Can Lead to Tragedy," *Scholastic Choices*, May 2013.
Matt McGrath	"Steroids Can Benefit Athletes for a Decade After Use," BBC News, October 29, 2013.
Brian Palmer	"The Long-Term Benefits of Juicing," *Slate*, March 30, 2012.
Tina Hesman Saey	"Gift of Steroids Keeps On Giving: Mouse Muscles Stay Juiced Long After Doping Ends," *Science News*, December 28, 2013.
Tatiana Siegel	"How Steroids Help Make Movie Muscles," *Hollywood Reporter*, August 2013.

OPPOSING
VIEWPOINTS®
SERIES

CHAPTER 3

How Effective Is Testing to Detect Performance-Enhancing Drugs?

Chapter Preface

In December 2013, Craig Reedie, president of the World Anti-Doping Agency (WADA), announced that £6 million ($10.1 million) in funds from the International Olympic Committee (IOC) may be earmarked to expand the agency's testing methods for performance-enhancing drugs (PEDs). "Now we will look at different approaches such as, can we use a lock of hair?" Reedie said. "This is a really exciting development and means we can look at approaches that in the past have been unaffordable."

Commonly used by employers and drug treatment programs, hair analysis is unique from other tests because of the characteristics of hair follicles. "Hair is a unique matrix because no active metabolism or excretion occurs within its structure to remove drugs once they have been deposited," explain Lata Gautam and Michael D. Cole, forensic science researchers, in a September 3, 2013, article in *Forensic Magazine*. Requiring between 90 and 120 strands of hair, the test provides a much longer window of detection—usually ninety days—and can reveal a history of drug use, depending on strand length. Obtaining a hair sample is also noninvasive, and detection occurs within seven to ten days after the drug was taken. "Provided the hair has not been cut, it may be easy to obtain a second sample if the results are inconclusive or challengeable," claim Gautam and Cole. Furthermore, tampering with a hair sample is unlikely because substances in it remain stable; if the head is shaved completely, hair follicles from other parts of the body can be used.

Testing for PEDs with hair analysis does have disadvantages, however. It is more expensive than urine testing and costs about the same as blood testing, between $100 to $150 per test. In addition, testing hair follicles is a time-intensive process and must be conducted in a laboratory. Cosmetic processing can also weaken the presence of substances in hair. "Therefore cosmetic history of a person must be considered in such cases while interpreting hair analysis results," advise Gautam and Cole. In the following chapter, the authors debate the effectiveness of PED testing in sports.

> "Information about the effectiveness of drug testing is hard to come by, as anti-doping scientists guard their secrets jealously."

How Performance-Enhancing Drug Testing Works, or Doesn't: Olympic Edition

John J. Ross

In the following viewpoint, John J. Ross asserts that testing for performance-enhancing drugs (PEDs) does not always work in catching athletes who use them. While the detection of steroids is a straightforward process, Ross insists that testing for steroids—which are used early in training—must be done when the athlete is out of competition, and some compounds are designed to mimic the biologic effects of testosterone. Furthermore, in screening for blood doping and human growth hormone, testing must also be conducted frequently when the athlete is out of competition, and the window of detection is narrow, he adds. The author is a hospitalist at Brigham and Women's Hospital in Boston, Massachusetts, as well as an assistant professor of medicine at Harvard Medical School and the author of Shakespeare's Tremor and Orwell's Cough: The Medical Lives of Famous Writers.

As you read, consider the following questions:

1. Who was the first Olympian to fail a drug test, as claimed by Ross?

2. According to the author, how may blood dopers attempt to avoid detection with athlete biological passports?

3. What are the anomalies in the National Football League's drug testing program, as stated by the author?

The Olympics have been playing catch-up with cheaters for a long time. Amphetamines and anabolic steroids were abused by athletes for decades before testing became available. In fact, the first Olympian who flunked a drug test ingested something that may not be performance-enhancing at all. In 1968, Swedish pentathlete Hans-Gunnar Liljenwall lost his bronze medal for drinking two beers to calm down before the pistol-shooting event.

Information about the effectiveness of drug testing is hard to come by, as anti-doping scientists guard their secrets jealously. However, by reviewing the medical literature, it is possible to piece together a status report on the cold war between dopers and scientists.

Steroids, Stimulants, and Diuretics: Detection of these compounds in urine samples is relatively straightforward and uses a two-step method. Liquid chromatography is first used to separate the compounds from one another. Then, in mass spectometry, each isolate is bombarded with electrons. This generates a unique molecular signature (mass spectrum) for each compound, based on its weight and electrical charge. However, these techniques have several limitations:

1. Steroids are often used to build muscle in the early months of training. Elite athletes must therefore be subject to frequent out-of-competition testing;

2. It is possible to make compounds that mimic the biological effects of testosterone, while lacking its distinctive (and easy to detect) steroid structure. These selective androgenic receptor modulators may be abused by athletes with access to unscrupulous chemists;

3. Elite athletes have taken to abusing pure testosterone in the form of short-acting skin gels. Testosterone is normally found in the urine, so additional analysis is necessary to determine whether or not it is natural. The urine is further tested for the ratio of testosterone (T) to its inactive relative, epitestosterone (E). The normal T/E ratio in urine is around 1:1. Ratios of up to 4:1 are allowed. The ineffably dumb Floyd Landis was stripped of his Tour de France title in 2006 for a T/E ratio of 12:1. Baseball player Ryan Braun was found to have a whopping T/E ratio of 30:1, but successfully appealed his 50-game suspension on the basis of delayed transporting of his urine specimen. Athletes may attempt to cover their tracks by taking epitestosterone, as well as testosterone, thus maintaining a normal T/E ratio. These cheaters may be detected by isotope analysis, which relies on the fact that manufactured testosterone usually contains different carbon isotopes from natural testosterone.

Advantage: Testers

Blood Doping: Athletes with more red blood cells carry more oxygen in the blood and thus have an edge in endurance sports. A scheme currently used by cyclists and other distance athletes is to inject synthetic erythropoietin (EPO), the hormone that signals the body to produce more red cells, daily for several weeks during the training season. One to three pints of blood are then drawn off, stored for several weeks, and reinfused back into the athlete just prior to the competition. Synthetic EPO will not be found in urine at the time of competition, as it will be long gone from the body. The only way to catch EPO users is frequent testing out of competition, and even this is not very effective. EPO is only detectable for 12–18 hours after use. Erythropoietin alfa and beta have the same protein structure as human EPO, but because they are made in hamster ovary cells, they have a different pattern of sugar binding (glycosylation) than natural EPO. However, erythropoietin delta, which is available in Europe, is made in human cells, and cannot be distinguished from natural EPO.

Reinfusion of stored blood may lead to positive tests for plastic residues (phthalates, which may be toxic to male gonads) in urine. However, as phthalate exposure is universal in modern societies, this test is probably not specific enough to be used as a basis for disqualifying athletes.

As EPO gets harder to test for, efforts have shifted to catching cheaters indirectly, by looking at changes over time in blood tests, or biomarkers, that suggest the use of EPO or other drugs. This concept is known as the athlete biological passport (ABP). The most useful biomarkers for blood doping are excessively high levels of hemoglobin and abnormal numbers of young red blood cells (reticulocytes), which may be high in active EPO users, or low in athletes that have just stopped using EPO. In one experiment, this approach was 58% effective in catching dopers, which is not bad, but not great either. The authors of this study noted that real-world cheaters will probably use lower doses of EPO, and will probably be tested less often. Blood dopers may also minimize changes in their biomarkers by getting blood just before an event and removing it immediately thereafter.

Advantage: Pick 'Em.

Human Growth Hormone (HGH): Natural HGH exists in the body as a mixture of related molecules of different weights,

or isoforms. Synthetic HGH, on the other hand, is a uniform preparation of the 22 kDa isoform. It is possible to detect HGH abuse if a blood test shows a predominance of the 22 kDa isoform, but the window for detection is narrow, only 22–36 hours, so frequent out-of-competition testing is again essential. (The NFL Players Association has questioned the standards for positive HGH tests established by the World

Anti-Doping Agency, arguing that HGH isoforms may differ in football players, compared to other athletes. The NFLPA proposes to define the normal range in football players by studying current HGH levels in football players, even though many of them may be abusing HGH. This is one of many anomalies in the NFL's supposedly awesome drug testing program, such as players being warned about no-warning drug tests.) There is a promising biomarkers approach to HGH detection. Blood levels of insulin-like growth factor 1 (IGF-1) and procollagen type 3 N-terminal peptide may remain elevated 2–4 weeks after HGH is stopped. It has just been announced that this testing approach will be ready for London 2012.

Advantage: Testers.

"Organizations which genuinely want to be monitored can be, while those that do not can easily avoid it."

The Ineffectiveness of Testing for Performance-Enhancing Drugs Is Due to Inefficient Support

World Anti-Doping Agency Working Group

The World Anti-Doping Agency (WADA) is an international organization working to lead a collaborative worldwide campaign against doping in sports. In the following viewpoint, a working group of WADA attributes a lack of support to the ineffectiveness of testing for performance-enhancing drugs (PEDs). First, the working group claims that WADA itself has weaknesses, such as its reputation as an "irritant" rather than an anti-doping leader and its tendency to avoid naming and shaming cheaters. The author then argues that sports organizations do not regard anti-doping as part of their business, resist testing by independent agencies, and are unwilling to investigate and use sanctions

Source: Report to WADA Executive Committee on Lack of Effectiveness of Testing Programs, prepared by Working Group established following Foundation Board Meeting of 18 May 2012. A full report can be found at the following link: https://wada-main-prod.s3.amazonaws.com/resources/files/2013-05-12-Lack-of-effectiveness-of-testing-WG-Report-Final.pdf. Reproduced by permission.

when doping violations occur. As for athletes, the author suggests that many do not publicly oppose doping, are single-minded in pursuing performance, and would not likely report doping if they encounter it.

As you read, consider the following questions:

1. What reluctance do sports organizations have in supporting effective anti-doping efforts, according to the viewpoint?

2. What does the author observe about the political appeal of anti-doping?

3. According to the author, what are athletes' concerns about whistleblowers?

Prior to the creation of WADA [World Anti-Doping Agency] in 1999, there was no concerted international effort directed at doping in sport. Few would disagree that there has been considerable progress in the fight against doping in sport, including scientific knowledge, awareness of the existence of a significant doping problem and an increased number of tests, both in and out of competition. Tests now exist for all EPO [erythropoietin], human growth hormone, homologous blood transfusion, testosterone, designer steroids and stimulants, SARMs [selective androgen receptor modulators] and other new hormones and metabolite modulators. Pre-WADA, approximately 150,000 tests were administered annually, compared with the current total of approximately 250,000. On the other hand, despite the significant increase in testing and the ability to detect more sophisticated substances, there has been no apparent statistical improvement in the number of positive results. Indeed, if the statistics regarding marijuana (approximately 500 AAFs [adverse analytical findings] per year), asthma medications (200) and glucocorticosteroids (234) for which therapeutic-use exemptions had probably been granted, are removed, less than 1% of the tests produce adverse analytical findings. There has not been any statistical improvement since about 1985. Many preliminary conclusions can be drawn from this, including that doped athletes are not tested at the right time, that they use undetectable substances or methods, that doped athletes avoid testing, plus a whole range of possibilities of organizational and/or human intervention or failure. . . .

The working group has considered why the testing portion of anti-doping programs does not seem to be working as effectively as it thinks it should, given the anecdotal and other evidence of doping at much higher levels than the number of positive cases would suggest. It has identified a number of issues that may help explain why testing is not as effective as it should be. The principal focus of the working group was on the detection of doping, as opposed, for example, to deterrents.

WADA

No review of the current (and future) situation would be complete without an assessment of WADA itself and whether it is doing the work that is expected of the organization. It may be that a significant realignment of its priorities and activities is required.

Weaknesses Observed

- Instead of WADA being recognized as the leader in the fight against doping in sport and supported by the stakeholders, it is viewed as an irritant, surrounded by stakeholders, some of which are self-interested or conflicted organizations

- Constantly increasing demands for activities, without concomitant budgetary support

- The result of the constantly increasing demands is that WADA does a number of core and non-core jobs rather poorly [if key document is the Code, then major focus should be on compliance with the Code]

- There are still issues as to whether WADA is a regulator or service provider

- Stakeholders are unwilling to impose sanctions when noncompliance is found

- WADA is unable to do more than report on noncompliance when aware

- Compliance issues are very low and unevenly applied

- Lack of interest on the part of many stakeholders in actually catching doping athletes

- In addition to quality assessments at the level of ADOs [anti-doping organizations], NADOs [national anti-doping organizations] and IFs [international federations], quality assessments for these organizations have not been implemented

- Lack of inclination on the part of WADA to name and shame

- Insufficient monitoring and receipt of required information

- No measurement of WADA's efficiency and effectiveness (goal assessment)

- There is no critical measurement of research funding [assessments of results and efficiency]. WADA has funded considerable non-useful research, reinventing the wheel, outside agencies, and other research not directed at increasing the efficacy of testing

- Increasing levels of complexity of Code and Standards (is downsizing documentation an option?)

- Organizations which genuinely want to be monitored can be, while those that do not can easily avoid it

International Sport Organizations

Sport organizations are responsible for adopting and enforcing the rules applicable to their sports and competitions. We need not address the technical rules applicable to each sport or competition. Our concern is the subset of rules relating to doping. Much of the former confusion arising from a broad variety of anti-doping rules has disappeared as a result of adoption of the Code. A considerable degree of latitude has been granted to sport organizations in the drafting of their anti-doping rules, with only certain identified provisions of the Code considered as mandatory. Some initial resistance to adoption of the Code was encountered, for example, from FIFA [international governing body of soccer], which considered its own anti-doping rules and procedures to be paramount, but the differences were eventually resolved following a reference to CAS [Court of Arbitration for Sport] regarding compliance.

Sport organizations involved include the IFs, the national federations (NFs) affiliated with the IFs, the NOCs [National Olympic Committees], and multisport organizations, such as the IOC [International Olympic Committee], regional associations of NOCs and continental organizations, whether of IFs or NOCs.

Anti-doping responsibilities rest initially with the IFs (which may delegate some of the responsibilities to their affiliated NFs), with the NOCs (when Olympic teams are involved), and with other organizations, depending on the rules governing particular competitions. Thus, for example, the IOC is the responsible authority during the Olympic Games and a specified period prior to the commencement of the games. IFs have a similar responsibility in respect of world championships.

Weaknesses Observed

- No incentive to catch dopers in the sport—anti-doping is not regarded as their core business (except perhaps for IFs facing a crisis)

- Reluctance to assume the costs of effective anti-doping efforts

- Focus is limited to technical Code compliance only, not to the effectiveness of anti-doping efforts

- Resistance to testing by independent organizations, with various rationalizations for such resistance

- Difficulty of access to athletes in certain countries

- Uneven commitment to rigorous compliance with anti-doping rules

- Lack of independence in many countries

- Reports of doping tests by many ADOs are untimely, incomplete and inconsistent

- There is no positive obligation to report instances/suspicions of doping, nor a readily available mechanism for doing so

- Unwillingness to investigate and use sanctions where systematic doping violations occur in a sport or in a country

- Resistance to higher standards of Code compliance

- Harsh treatment of whistleblowers

- Very little adoption of the athlete biological profile (ABP) system, despite its usefulness to reduce overall testing and to increase target testing; while blood profiles have been around for years, there are few experts in steroid profiles

- Lack of systematic follow-up regarding serious accusations (whether from athletes, officials or third parties) of doping and cover-ups of doping; some from lack of inclination, some from lack of appropriate governance process. . . .

Governments

The involvement of governments in the fight against doping in sport was a major step forward when WADA was created in 1999 on the basis of 50-50 governance. This was reinforced with the adoption and subsequent ratification of the Convention. The initial few years of WADA's existence were quite exciting, as the Code was developed and the negotiations leading to the adoption of the Convention proceeded. Governments demonstrated their commitment by sending ministers to WADA meetings, who took an active interest in its activities and set the tone for the ambitious new organization. Governments worked hard and effectively to determine the continental levels of representation on the WADA Foundation Board and the sourcing of the governmental portion of financial contributions to WADA, also on a continental basis.

As WADA has moved from its formative stages to the ongoing operational fight against doping in sport, ministerial enthusiasm has waned and fewer ministers are attending the WADA meetings. Whatever political appeal anti-doping may have had seems to have worn off and more and more states now send civil servants as their representatives. Many of the latter seem to measure their organizational success by how they are able to limit increases in budget contributions or to reducing such contributions, rather than to the effective accomplishment of the WADA mission. The Olympic Movement, for its part, shows no desire to argue for increased funding.

Weaknesses Observed

- Lack of political commitment to fight against doping

- Universal calls for increased activities by WADA, coupled with demonstrated unwillingness to provide adequate resources

- Limited access to certain countries for purposes of out-of-competition (OOC) testing

- Lack of any positive suggestions for improvements in the fight against doping in sport

- Active interference in the effectiveness of anti-doping activities (e.g., data protection issues continually raised by a small group of civil servants, designed to prevent effective worldwide activities)

- No meaningful monitoring process for compliance with international convention (total self-reporting)

- Intimations that in certain countries there is state-sponsored or state-protected doping

- Unwillingness to share doping-related information (more blessed to receive than to give)

- Unwillingness to put into effect laws relating to trafficking, distribution, etc., which is a Convention undertaking (see also contaminated meat and access to clenbuterol)

- Lack of independence of certain NADOs

- Lack of international cooperation and harmonization of legislation

- Increased availability of doping substances (e.g., Internet)

- Some governments have impeded the investigation and follow-up on doping activities, as well as the sharing of information...
- Unwillingness of governments to engage professional codes of conduct
- Resistance in some countries to access CAS
- Lack of structured education programs (including educating children on the proper use of medications, values)....

Athletes

Athletes are at the centre of the doping hub. It is the athlete who is directly affected by doping, whether as perpetrator or one cheated by a doped athlete. Doping, with the exception of mislabelled innocuous supplements, is very seldom an accident. It is normally a deliberate plan to obtain an unfair advantage over competitors who abide by the applicable rules—or, at best, an attempt to keep up with those believed to be doping. It is cheating. It may also be dangerous cheating.

Weaknesses Observed

- Values-based education (from many perspectives) is too weak—affects athletes, hence identification of a weakness, even though the responsibility rests with governments and NADOs
- Athletes are less inclined than one might expect to identify doping when they encounter it
- Relatively few athletes take a publicly strong position against doping
- Most athletes are single-minded in their pursuit of performance and have no useful knowledge of doping, nor to whom they can speak [if they are naïve, they know nothing; if they are doping, they will not talk]

- Lack of information on how doped athletes are/were able to survive the testing system without detection (e.g., outside pre-knowledge, micro-dosages, failure to observe provision of urine samples)

- Athletes seldom offer suggestions, based on their experience, of how to improve testing and other methods of identifying dopers and enablers

- Athletes are concerned that whistleblowers are treated more harshly than the dopers and that they will be punished and isolated if they come forward

- Similarly, clean athletes are concerned that whistleblowers who have doped can get treated too softly

- Rationalization of reasons for doping indicates that the "values" aspect among athletes is not as strong as one might hope

- There is no positive obligation to report instances/suspicions of doping, nor a generally available hotline for the purpose

- IFs generally discourage whistleblowing on the part of athletes

- Doping athletes from nations that ignore, condone or support doping programs know they will likely be tested if they leave their (certain) countries, so they do not travel, while doping athletes from nations that have well-developed anti-doping programs travel to testing "havens" overseas to avoid being tested at home

- Athletes who dope (and/or their entourages) know how to manipulate ABPs

- Young athletes may not know what they have been given

- Athletes who dope (and/or their entourages) know how to manipulate plasma and fluid volumes by intravenous or oral intake

- Athletes who dope (and/or their entourages) keep up with the research WADA funds

- High value of athletic success attracts government attention, brings notoriety and pressures to succeed

- Athletes often poorly educated on drugs, medications and supplements, particularly younger athletes when they are first entering international sport

> "Blood testing is a political ruse at the
> very best."

Urine Testing:
The Focal Point for All
Performance-Enhancing
Drug Testing

American Swimming Magazine

American Swimming Magazine is published by the American Swimming Coaches Association. In the following viewpoint, the author contends that efforts to improve the detection of performance-enhancing drugs (PEDs) should focus on urine testing. Blood testing for human growth hormone (HGH) is impractical, limited, and not scientifically sound, argues the author. Moreover, citing an interview with an expert on testing, the author insists that urine testing, unlike blood testing, directly proves when an athlete has used erythropoietin (EPO). While cheaper and more convenient for testers, blood testing is invasive and does not fit in with athletes' lifestyles, the author adds.

As you read, consider the following questions:

1. What statistic does the author provide for the effectiveness of blood testing for HGH?

2. What does blood testing for EPO tell testers, according to the viewpoint?

3. Why is urine testing more costly, as stated in the viewpoint?

The Manny Pacquiao–Floyd Mayweather Jr. debacle has led to an incredible amount of posturing and, as a result, misinformation and incomplete information. This posturing has been under the guise of a campaign for a drug-free sport, something we all favor. But the posturing obscures the scientific truth.

First, the best experts in the field report there is no good test for HGH [human growth hormone]. At present, there is no urine test that works. And Dr. Don H. Catlin, head of the UCLA [University of California, Los Angeles] Olympic Analytical Lab and for many years one of the most knowledgeable experts in the area—possibly the most knowledgeable—has stated that he believes blood testing is impractical. He points out that, out of 1,500 blood tests, only one came back positive for HGH despite a well-founded suspicion that HGH use is far more prevalent. In part, this is because the detection limit is short, about 24 hours. In other words, the athlete would have had to use HGH within approximately 24 hours of the test to actually be caught.

Further, the one athlete who was "busted" for HGH after testing admitted to use. Many scientists do not believe that, if it came to proving the scientific validity of the WADA [World Anti-Doping Agency] drug testing protocols for HGH in court or before an arbitrator, the results would survive legal challenge based upon scientific validity. Dr. Peter Sonksen, a pioneer in the field of HGH testing, says "There's very little new [data verifying the WADA test], and I think it would be quite easy for a lawyer to draw 'cart and horses through it in court.'" This charge is echoed by epidemiologist Dr. Charles E. Yesalis of Penn State, who contends that the scientific data to back the testing protocols is insufficient to the point of being "almost criminal."

Dr. Catlin has said flatly that the method of testing used by WADA "alone doesn't work. It's political. The whole thing is political."

Further, anyone who has ever been involved in Olympic-style testing knows its flaws and limitations. Blood tests, if done randomly, are exceedingly infrequent. Athletes who are subject to in-and-out-of-competition testing go years with no blood tests (though urine testing is another matter).

Further, unannounced Olympic-style testing involves a level of intrusion that few professional athletes can or would countenance. As an example, spur-of-the-moment activities must be reported to WADA, according to the rules, 24 hours in advance. If an athlete decides to go to the shore on a sunny day, to go to assist a friend, or any of the plethora of activities of which we all partake every week, it must be reported to WADA in advance. This is tough enough to do with college athletes, more or less captive on campuses, and virtually impossible with professionals with normal lives. In recognition of its difficulty, athletes are permitted to miss three tests due to unavailability before action is taken. That brings us right back to the testing protocols. If HGH is detectable for only 24 hours, all an athlete needs to do is to arrange to be unavailable for testing the following day. Chances are overwhelmingly small that any test will be taken the following day. But if one is to be taken, the athlete can simply make himself unavailable that day without penalty.

Further, the Olympic process is slow. The example of one Olympic-level athlete is illustrative. Jessica Hardy, a swimmer, gave a urine sample on July 4, 2008. It was not until July 23 that she was notified of the failed drug test. She initially challenged the result and thus had the right to a hearing. That hearing began on August 1, 2008, when she withdrew her

The Specimen Standard in Testing

Regardless of its limitations or the complications it imposes, urine remains the specimen standard in sports drug testing. Laboratories have extensive scientific basis for the testing methodology and scientists have developed extremely sophisticated instruments and procedures using urine specimens to effectively detect many of the more common substances currently being abused by athletes.

Joel E. Houglum and Gary L. Harrelson,
Principles of Pharmacology for Athletic Trainers.
Second Edition. Thorofare, NJ: SLACK Incorporated, 2011.

challenge. Thus it took approximately three weeks before she was even notified (resulting from the need to test the "B" sample) and four weeks before the matter was resolved. The Hardy matter involved a steroid with established scientific validity and an admission. It was claimed by Dr. Sonksen there are flaws in the methodology for HGH testing, a legal challenge will take very considerably longer.

Whether Jessica Hardy was allowed to compete or not, the Olympics were going to proceed and her situation had no impact on its promotion. However, the same is not true of a boxing promotion. We have seen far too many situations when results from an "A" sample and from a "B" sample do not correspond (thus both need to be tested) and even situations from reputable labs where contamination, later discovered, made results unreliable. This is why the due process of a hearing is necessary. By the time this is completed, a boxing event will have either already taken place or been irretrievably destroyed.

Drs. Catlin, Sonksen and Yesalis are not advocates for abuse of drugs in sport. To the contrary, they are respected researchers who have done much to attempt to eliminate performance-enhancing drugs in sport. Dr. Catlin heads the most respected drug-testing laboratory in the United States and developed the test which broke the BALCO scandal [referring to a scandal involving Bay Area Laboratory Cooperative, a business that provided anabolic steroids to professional athletes]. Dr. Sonksen is a fellow of the Royal [College] of Physicians with some 315 scientific publications, many on this very topic. Dr. Yesalis coauthored the first comprehensive surveys of teen steroid use.

Catlin, Sonksen, and others are working on legitimate, more reliable tests for HGH. While it may appear politically correct and provide a good "sound bite" to jump on the bandwagon for drug-free sports, the truth is that the blood testing suggested for HGH is, at best, limited and impractical and at worst scientifically suspect. Efforts should be toward developing tests that work and then implementing them; not in pretending that there are good and generally accepted scientifically valid testing techniques when there are not.

Also here is an excerpt from an interview of Dr. Catlin, considered the forefather of PED testing that you will find very interesting and testimony to both the economics and politics surrounding PED testing.

QUESTION:

1. EPO [erythropoietin] is a naturally occurring substance in the body. Could an athlete who lives at altitude or has great genetics and thus might have more EPO in their body naturally than a normal person, test positive for EPO?

No. Currently, to be convicted of an EPO offense, athletes must test positive for EPO with the urine EPO test. The urine EPO test is not an indirect test that detects unusually high EPO levels. Rather, it is a direct test that detects the actual presence of recombinant EPO (EPO from a source outside the body). Thus, it would be foolish for an athlete to argue that the test was just showing a naturally high level of natural EPO. As Dr. Catlin said to us, with the urine EPO test, the testers "see a footprint of the (recombinant EPO) molecule."

The World Anti-Doping [Agency] report of March 11, 2003, evaluating the urine EPO test concluded, "The urine EPO test is the only existing test to directly evaluate and prove the EPO abuse of athletes."

2. I've heard a lot about using both a blood and urine test to detect EPO use. Doesn't an athlete have to test positive for EPO on both the blood and urine test to be considered a doper?

No.

Blood testing has received a lot of attention because it is a new concept in the drug-testing world. There is a blood test for EPO use, but it is only an indirect test that can be used as a screening measure to save money by determining whether the urine EPO test needs to be conducted. All the blood test does is tell the testers that the athlete has an unusual blood profile that warrants further investigation. The abnormal profile could be caused by the use of EPO, some other blood-boosting drug, or just be explained by the athlete being a genetic freak or living at altitude. The testers then perform the urine EPO test to determine whether artificial EPO is the cause of the abnormality.

The blood test does not have to be done in order for the athlete to test positive for EPO.

3. If the blood test doesn't have to be performed, then why does it exist? Not only do you say it is unnecessary, but it seems quite invasive and expensive to test athletes' blood when a simple urine test could be done.

Believe it or not, the blood EPO test is much cheaper than the urine EPO test. The blood test costs somewhere in the ballpark of $60, whereas the urine test costs approximately $400 per test. The reason for this is that conducting the urine EPO test takes up a lot of the time of the technicians in the lab (sometimes up to two or three days). Thus, the blood EPO test can be used in situations to save money.

It would be very expensive to conduct urine EPO tests on all athletes at $400 a pop. Thus the blood EPO test can be used to determine which athletes are most likely to be on EPO, and then the urine EPO test can be administered on this smaller subsample. . . .

Blood testing, although cheaper, is admittedly invasive, and non-conducive to a pro athlete's lifestyle usually having at least two training camps. . . .

Urine tests have been and remain the focal point for all PED detection. Blood testing is a political ruse at the very best; the WADA has always been under the umbrella of suspicion.

As human beings, we are far too quick to jump on the most convenient bandwagon and wave our flags of discontent before the facts will out.

"Hopes are high among sports federations and anti-doping agencies that the biological passport will close some of the biggest loopholes that have let cheaters slip into . . . major events."

The Biological Passport

Susan Gilbert

Susan Gilbert is the public affairs and communications manager for the Hastings Center, a nonprofit bioethics organization. In the following viewpoint, she declares that the biological passport, which electronically profiles and monitors an athlete's test results for the effects—not the presence—of performance-enhancing drugs (PEDs), is an effective way to identify doping. Gilbert insists that numerous loopholes in drug tests, such as a short window of detection or use of an undetectable substance, can be closed by biological passports. Furthermore, the approach acknowledges athletes who do not use PEDs and promotes change in the culture of sports and doping, she maintains.

As you read, consider the following questions:

1. How are false positives prevented in biological passports, as stated by Gilbert?

Susan Gilbert, "The Biological Passport," *Hastings Center Report*, vol. 40. no 2, 2010, pp. 18–19.

2. What biological passport guidelines does the World Anti-Doping Agency call for, as described by Gilbert?

3. According to the viewpoint, how would a voluntary biological passport program change the culture of sports?

The gatekeepers of fair sport have a whole new way to identify doping: the "athlete biological passport." An approach that has evolved over the last several years, it is an electronic record of test results of the lingering *effects* of banned substances in the body, rather than the substances themselves. Like a valid passport required for entry into foreign countries, a valid (clean) biological passport is now required for many athletes to gain entry into elite competitions. Hopes are high among sports federations and anti-doping agencies that the biological passport will close some of the biggest loopholes that have let cheaters slip into the Olympics, the Tour de France, and other major events.

Standard sports doping tests look for drugs like designer steroids or synthetic erythropoietin (EPO), a hormone injected to increase endurance by increasing oxygen in the blood. One gaping loophole in such tests is that some drugs, like EPO, can only be detected in the body for a few days. But the effects of the drugs last for a week or more, increasing the odds that users will get caught. Another loophole is that banned substances, for a variety of reasons, are sometimes impossible to detect: they can be designed to elude specific tests, new substances can be made for which there are no tests, and a genetic trait—missing copies of a gene called UGT2B17, which makes testosterone soluble in urine—renders testosterone doping invisible to conventional urine tests. (The absence of this gene is strongly related to ethnicity: 81 percent of Asians, 22 percent of Africans, and 10 percent of Caucasians are missing both copies.) Looking for the physiological footprints left by such drugs, rather than the particular culprits, should reduce these problems.

The Biological Passport and Cycling

Many newly developed pharmaceuticals are unlikely to be detectable by conventional tests and thus can be discovered only through their effects on the body. For this reason, the so-called biological passport, a longitudinal monitoring system for blood values, was introduced for all professional cyclists. In contrast to the previous system, where a fixed limit for certain values was used (e.g., haematocrit 50 per cent or haemoglobin concentration 17 $g \cdot dl^{-1}$), the biological passport calculates individual reference values for each rider for several variables using an elaborate software system based on Bayesian statistics. These reference ranges are based on each athlete's previous results, thereby setting individual thresholds for each of the blood test parameters. After its introduction in 2008, 10,603 controls for the biological passport were conducted during the following year.

James Hopker and Simon Jobson,
Performance Cycling: the Science of Success.
London, UK: Bloomsbury Publisher, 2012.

A handful of sports federations have used the biological passport on a trial basis, but it is becoming more widespread because the World Anti-Doping Agency, which leads the international effort against banned sports enhancement, just released guidelines on its use. The U.S. Anti-Doping Agency and similar groups in the United Kingdom and Norway have adopted the passport for elite athletes in those countries. Under WADA's guidelines, testing occurs unannounced several times a year throughout an athlete's career. Initial readings establish a normal baseline for each athlete. Variations consistent with use of EPO, illicit blood transfusions, and other methods of increasing blood oxygen can trigger an investigation. To prevent false positives, information is collected about legitimate activities that can affect the readings such as blood donation during the previous six months, medications or supplements taken, and training.

Already, the passport has led to investigations of a speed-skating champion and five cyclists. Last year, the speed skater, Claudia Pechstein, was found guilty of doping and was banned by the International Skating Union from competing for two years (although she won an appeal in a Swiss court, which allowed her to compete in the Olympic Oval in Utah last December). At press time, cases against the five cyclists were pending with the International Cycling Union.

David Howman, director general of WADA, hopes that the biological passport will reduce the false negatives that plague the fight against sports doping. "There are many athletes, like Marion Jones, who were tested for years and were never found to be cheating," he said. Jones, a track-and-field champion, admitted in 2007 to using "the clear," a steroid formulated by the Bay Area Laboratory Co-operative, known as BALCO, to elude steroid testing. Howman believes that the passport approach will identify athletes like Jones. For now, WADA's guidelines call for testing the blood for nine markers that change with oxygen enhancement, including hematocrit, hemoglobin, and red blood cells count. But WADA is aiming to expand its biological passport guidelines to include the effects of synthetic steroids. USADA used the passport to look for evidence of anabolic steriods and prohibited hormones in a pilot program in 2008. "The intention is to have not just a blood profile but a total body profile," Howman said.

In addition to identifying more of the athletes who use banned performance enhancers, Howman envisions the biological passport rewarding the athletes who don't. In that sense, he sees the passport as a more ethical approach to fighting sports doping. "It gives clean athletes a better opportunity to say, 'I'm clean,'" he said.

The idea of rewarding the honest athletes appeals to Don Catlin, a leading researcher on sports doping who, among many other achievements, helped expose the BALCO scandal by identifying "the clear." Catlin has long supported the biological passport concept because of its potential to change the culture of sports by acknowledging athletes who do *not* dope. But he believes that the best way to do this is with a voluntary program. Such a program would naturally attract clean athletes, whose reward for volunteering would be public recognition—by the press and sports federations—that they really are clean.

A voluntary program would have other important advantages, says Catlin, founder of the UCLA Olympic Analytical Laboratory, the first anti-doping lab in the United States, and now chief executive of Anti-Doping Research, a nonprofit agency in Los Angeles. If the athletes consented to have their test samples used for research, it would improve scientific understanding of the range of readings that are normal. "To really reduce false negatives, you've got to have a lot of data on a lot of people to know where to draw the line," he said. "We're not there yet." Just as important, he said, the voluntary approach would make athletes partners in the anti-doping process, instead of being treated as adversaries.

But support for a voluntary program has not caught on. USADA tried it last year and had twelve volunteers, including Michael Phelps. "The program sent a powerful and positive message to athletes and the public that performance-enhancing drugs have no place in sport," wrote Erin Hannan, a USADA spokeswoman, in an email message. She said it also strengthened the science behind the testing protocols. But culture change takes time, and the need to secure the borders of fair sport is urgent—especially now, in an Olympic year. It's easy to see why USADA and similar groups have embraced mandatory passport testing.

"In theory, the biological passport news is a step in the right direction. In practice? Well, that remains to be seen."

Biological Passports May Not Be Effective in Detecting Performance-Enhancing Drugs

Blair Henley

In the following viewpoint, Blair Henley claims that the biological passport—which tracks and compiles an athlete's test results to identify the effects of performance-enhancing drugs (PEDs)—is promising in theory but problematic in practice. Placing it in the context of tennis, Henley persists that implementing a biological passport program would inflate anti-doping costs and significantly increase the number of blood tests a player would have to take. Furthermore, some tennis officials are in denial of doping and are not likely to invest time and money in creating an effective program. The author is an assistant coach for the Rice University tennis team and contributes to Tennis Now *and* World Tennis Magazine.

As you read, consider the following questions:

1. What is Henley's opinion of the International Tennis Federation's (ITF) initiation of the biological passport program?

2. What does Don Catlin state about urine testing and biological passports?

3. What is a positive outcome of the ITF's proposing a biological passport program, in Henley's view?

Last fall [in 2012] before the U.S. Anti-Doping Agency's case against [former cyclist] Lance Armstrong exploded onto every newspaper headline in the free world and before big-name players (plus [retired tennis player] Christophe Rochus) had their say on the topic, the possibility of doping in tennis was simply not discussed. Journalists certainly weren't writing about it, and the athletes themselves appeared content with the status quo. In the interest of preserving the fragile "tennis is clean" ideal, analysis of glaring loopholes and inconsistencies in the ITF's [International Tennis Federation's] anti-doping program was avoided like a [tennis player Roger] Federer inside-out forehand.

What a difference a few months make.

Now just about everyone has an opinion on whether or not the ITF, responsible for growing and promoting the sport of tennis, is also doing a good job of policing its headliners. With the bandwagon suddenly rolling, fans, media, players, and even the Grand Slams hopped on, all agreeing on something most of them would have denied one year ago: the ITF anti-doping program is ineffective. And, as exciting as it is to think the ITF is finally waking up and smelling the testosterone cream, the newly established open dialogue on the doping subject will likely do more good in the immediate future than any of the ITF's proposed changes.

At this point, the criticisms of the current system have been rehashed more than the state of [tennis player Rafael] Nadal's fickle patella tendon. In addition to the obvious conflict of interests facing the ITF, there are far too few out-of-competition tests and blood tests. The recently released anti-doping statistics for 2012 reflect a marginal increase in each of these categories compared to the stats from 2011, but don't get too excited. The ITF actually administered fewer blood tests this year than they did in 2006; a fact conveniently overshadowed by the simultaneous announcement of the ITF's plans to implement a biological passport system.

A Step in the Right Direction—in Theory

In theory, the biological passport news is a step in the right direction. In practice? Well, that remains to be seen. While it makes sense to establish blood profiles that provide a baseline with which to analyze subsequent drug tests, implementation is not so straightforward. The additional funding from the Grand Slams plus the financial boost from the ATP [Association of Tennis Professionals] and WTA [Women's Tennis Association] tours will reportedly inflate the ITF anti-doping budget to around $3.5 million, up from just under $2 million. But then consider that simply establishing a player's profile would require a massive increase (think quadruple) in the current number of blood tests.

At first glance it would seem that even a half-baked passport program would, by nature of its existence, greatly improve the scope of the current testing infrastructure. But it appears all passport-related blood tests will be scheduled (i.e., the players know they are coming). Will the ITF increase blood tests fourfold to build each profile, and then pay for unannounced, out-of-competition tests on top of that?

The ITF's proposed improvements made for great publicity, but with no apparent timeline or strategy for initiating the program, one can't help but wonder if it's a diversion tactic designed to halt a steady stream of criticism. After all, the news is coming from ITF president Francesco Ricci Bitti who has volunteered gems like this:

"I am not as pretentious as to think that we can catch all cheats. But I am confident that tennis is a clean sport."

And this:

"I say we can only be proud, because we started very early in anti-doping, and we believe we have a quality program."

And this, in reference to players' claims that they are being tested less now than they were several years ago:

"I don't think they are right. But it's a bit strange. They change their minds a lot."

Remarks from Stuart Miller, head of the ITF's anti-doping arm, have been equally unsettling. Miller has insisted multiple times that tennis is a skill sport in which players wouldn't necessarily benefit from systematic doping. If Ricci Bitti and Miller aren't convinced there was a problem in the first place, it seems unlikely they will invest the necessary time and money in creating a new anti-doping culture.

Perhaps that's why Don Catlin, widely regarded as a founder of modern drug testing, described the move as "grandstanding." Catlin also said the increased budget is still too low, and tennis is "far behind other sports" in its testing efforts.

"I would tell them not to bother," he told the *Guardian*. "They're better off to increase the number of tests they do rather than spend it all on the passport. Doubling or tripling urine tests would be of more value than starting a passport because you need such a long lead-in. You need data over four or five years."

Addressing the Inadequacy of the System

It appears the initial optimism regarding the ITF's seemingly newfound resolve may have been a bit premature, but all is not lost. Doping talk is now as trendy as Rafa's new short-

shorts, and that's a good thing. Players are becoming educated on the inadequacy of the system charged with keeping tennis clean, and the mainstream media is covering the transition.

While players and writers can't accuse unless they've personally seen [insert star athlete here] hiding under a massage table self-administering a post-match dose of EPO [erythropoietin], they should never shy away from discussion because a topic is considered taboo. In this case, questions have promoted change, if minor, for the ITF anti-doping program. The proof is in the passport. Now if only the ITF would improve organizational transparency by announcing positive tests and provisional suspensions immediately after they happen. . . .

When it comes to public discourse and sports reporting, *Grantland*'s Bill Simmons summed it up in his recent essay "Daring to Ask the PED Question":

"What are we hiding from? Who are we protecting? What's the difference between wondering if [star running back, Adrian] Peterson had help with his comeback and wondering if he's going to break [football player] [Eric] Dickerson's record? Either way, we're just speculating, right? Well, that's what we do. . . . WE SPECULATE ON STUFF!!!!!!!"

> "Despite the dire, rights-free lives of many athletes today, what has been the response of the human-rights lobby? That's right: silence."

In Defence of the Rights of Sportsmen

Klaus Wivel

In the following viewpoint, Klaus Wivel argues that anti-doping efforts in sports have become a crusade infringing on human rights. He persists that athletes must report their whereabouts to doping authorities at all times, be available for testing each day, be subjected to intrusive procedures to collect blood and urine samples, and face punishments and media scrutiny that can ruin their careers. Moreover, he adds, athletes are very rarely acquitted when testing produces false positives and, when contesting a test result, are required under strict liability to prove that the banned substance involuntarily entered the body. Based in New York City, Wivel is a reporter for Weekendavisen, *a Danish weekly cultural newspaper.*

As you read, consider the following questions:

1. What happened during testing that made a German athlete give up her career, as claimed by Wivel?

Klaus Wivel, "In Defence of the Rights of Sportsmen," *spiked*, September 14, 2011.

2. According to Wivel, why are the World Anti-Doping Agency's anti-doping efforts a failure?

3. What does Michael A. Hiltzik allege about anti-doping authorities?

In the name of an international war against drugs, a large number of people are currently forced to live under a system of surveillance that is so thorough and so intrusive that you would expect human-rights campaign groups like Amnesty International to be up in arms about it. Who are these oppressed people? Why is their treatment eliciting no Amnesty-style outrage? The answer, it seems, is one and the same: they're not proper people, they're sports people.

Take a look for yourselves at the *1984*-style regime these athletes have to live under. First, they are required to keep the doping authorities informed of their whereabouts at all times, and second they have to be available for testing for at least one hour each day. Athletes who fail three times to notify the authorities of their whereabouts risk a two-year ban from their sport—enough to wreck a career. In effect, athletes live on a leash. One of the most prominent anti-doping crusaders, physiologist Michael Ashenden, has even suggested that athletes should be obliged to carry a GPS device so that doping authorities can monitor their movements 24 hours a day.

Athletes are also expected to provide blood and urine samples upon request. While giving urine samples, male athletes have to lower their underwear down to their knees and roll up their t-shirts. This is to prove to the official that the urine sample really does come from the athlete in question. In the past, there have been instances of athletes submitting fake samples, most notably the Tour de France rider who was subsequently congratulated on his pregnancy.

Naturally, most athletes feel extremely uncomfortable with all this. At a recent seminar at Aarhus University's Institute of Sports in Denmark, sports psychologist Anne-Marie Elbe mentioned the case of a young, talented German athlete who wasn't able to perform her mandatory urine test in front of doping officials despite her drinking several litres of water and waiting for hours. Eventually, the test was cancelled. Half a year later, the athlete gave up her career. She didn't want to put herself through the humiliation again.

Then there's the Danish cyclist Michael Rasmussen. Recently, a doping official turned up at his home in Italy demanding a urine sample. Rasmussen couldn't urinate immediately because he had just done so before the doping control officer showed up. However, shortly after the officer's arrival he felt nature calling once more. Yet he wasn't allowed to do this in private as the control officer would have to record a failed test. This would likely mean a lifetime ban for Rasmussen who had already served a two-year ban for failing to report his whereabouts.

It was the second time in two years that Rasmussen had to accept this type of intrusion. One can only wonder at how many other professional athletes out there have experienced the same kind of humiliating treatment. Rasmussen later filed a complaint with the Danish anti-doping authorities, saying: 'I wish all of you had to shit in front of a German in your own house. It is not a pleasant experience.'

It is widely known that many top athletes are able to circumvent the doping controls, and almost half of those who do get caught are convicted of taking drugs that are not really performance-enhancing at all, like cannabis and cocaine. The rest of the doping offenders are mostly hobby weightlifters who test positive for steroids in fitness centres that anti-doping authorities (at least in Denmark) are allowed to control. Although steroids certainly are extremely unhealthy, it is difficult to see exactly who these bodybuilders are cheating, other than themselves. These muscle men are pumping iron for image enhancement, not for competitive reasons.

The anti-doping crusade has become an industry that far exceeds the world of professional competitive sports. The cases used to justify its growth and the severe infringements on athletes' privacy are widely known. From Ben Johnson's disqualification as Olympic 100 metres champion in 1988 to cycling's Festina scandal of 1998, the world of professional sports has been haunted by athletes who have tried to take shortcuts to victory. The World Anti-Doping Agency (WADA) was subsequently established in 1999 to coordinate the international efforts to 'clean up' sports.

Twelve years on, it is apparent that WADA is a big failure. Doping officials rarely find offenders at the top levels of sports. In fact, the police have been far more effective in rooting out the drug dealers, even though the police, too, have probably just scratched the surface. So WADA now wants to work in close cooperation with Interpol.

In truth, the anti-doping authorities have long been in cahoots with lawmakers and law enforcers. Back in 1999, the US Clinton administration, which was then very publicly committed to the war on drugs, demanded that cocaine and cannabis be put on the WADA list. This despite the fact that medical experts concluded that cannabis is the opposite of performance-enhancing and that cocaine only works as an enhancer if it is taken one-and-a-half hours before competition, and even then it isn't very effective.

Most doping offences are committed by young athletes who smoked a joint or snorted coke at a party. And although these blunders have nothing to do with their sports and everything to do with being young, they will still get suspended for months or even years in the case of cocaine. During this time they are not allowed to compete in any sport and may even be banned from sports grounds. Get caught twice with cocaine in your blood and you can never compete again. On top of that, your reputation is usually butchered by the tabloid press.

Sports journalists have a field day every time a sinner is caught but few question whether doping convictions are reasonable. As the Pulitzer Prize–winning American journalist Michael A Hiltzik told me last year: 'Every time an athlete is accused the debate plummets. . . . Sports journalists are not in the habit of dealing with complex issues. Sciences, law, psychology—they are very uncomfortable with all that. This is why athletes who are charged on an extremely thin basis are razed to the ground by the media. Once charged you lose everything.'

In 2006, Hiltzik wrote two damning articles about WADA for the *Los Angeles Times*. He mentioned a string of examples of grotesque convictions. For instance, there was the then 17-year-old Italian swimmer Giorgia Squizzato who, during a competition, used some antibiotic cream that her mother had bought for her to treat a foot infection. The cream contained a steroid that was on the WADA list of banned substances. Although the judge of the arbitration case acknowledged that the substance could not have improved her performance, Squizzato received a one-year suspension.

Only in very rare cases has an athlete who tested positive been acquitted. Hiltzik showed that thousands of athletes are subject to a system where 'anti-doping authorities act as prosecutors, judge and jury, enforcing rules that they have written, punishing violations based on sometimes questionable scientific tests that they develop and certify themselves, while barring virtually all outside appeals or challenges'.

One prime example is the curious case of the Danish soccer player Jesper Münsberg. Ahead of a friendly [game] for his club Næstved in February 2008, long-term asthmatic Münsberg was suffering from a bad cold. So, just before kickoff, he took several deep puffs on his asthma spray, something Anti-Doping Denmark had always permitted, even though the spray contained salbutamol, which is on WADA's list of banned substances.

Treating Athletes as Autonomous Beings Worthy of Respect

How far a right to privacy should extend is currently being debated in the medical ethics literature, and the sporting world could benefit from paying attention to this discourse. Privacy is a frequently discussed topic in the contemporary bioethics literature because of the role it plays in treating people as autonomous beings worthy of respect.... Since drug testing and genetic testing of athletes involve procedures and tests that originated in the medical context, it is important to note the reverence that respect for privacy holds in the bioethics and medical ethics fields.

Sarah Teetzel, "Respecting Privacy in Detecting Illegitimate Enhancements in Athletes," in The Ethics of Sports Medicine. *Eds. Claudio M. Tamburrini and Torbjörn Tännsjö. New York: Routledge, 2009.*

That cold winter evening, inspectors from Anti-Doping Denmark paid Münsberg a visit. The test he took showed that the amount of salbutamol in his urine was more than one-and-a-half times above the permitted limit. Initially the Danish Sports Confederation doping committee dismissed the case. But in June 2008 WADA asked it to look at the matter again. Once more the case was dismissed. WADA appealed to the Court of Arbitration for Sport (CAS).

In February 2009 Münsberg was flown to Oslo where he underwent a three-day-long series of experiments under the supervision of WADA's Norwegian inspectors. The experiments demonstrated that Münsberg was able once again to obtain an almost equally high level of salbutamol in the blood just by taking several puffs on his asthma spray. With these results Münsberg and his Danish team of lawyers went to Lausanne to try to convince CAS. It was all in vain. The three judges sentenced the Dane to six months' suspension in November 2009.

As the chairman of the Danish players association, Anders Øland remarked: 'For elite athletes fighting WADA—with the reverse burden of proof and with WADA's many resources—it is a David-versus-Goliath fight. The demands of the accused to prove their innocence are completely unreasonable and are having great economic and personal consequences.'

In any normal civic court, anti-doping authorities wouldn't stand a chance of winning these cases. That's why the world of sports has introduced the extremely questionable judicial concept of 'strict liability'. This means that it is not up to the prosecution to prove that a forbidden substance entered the body voluntarily. Instead it is up to the athlete to prove that a forbidden substance has entered the body involuntarily. In other words: you're guilty until proven innocent.

Michael Joyner, professor of anaesthesiology and expert in EPO and blood doping, put it well when he said: "The war against doping is like a small version of the war on terror. When you wage a battle that destroys the values you claim to defend, your loss is twice as fatal."

Yet curiously, despite the dire, rights-free lives of many athletes today, what has been the response of the human rights lobby? That's right: silence.

Periodical and Internet Sources Bibliography

The following articles have been selected to supplement the diverse views presented in this chapter.

Warren Cornwall	"The Secret to a Bulletproof Antidoping Test?," *New York Times*, February 25, 2014.
Simon Cox	"Athletics Drug-Testing Report a Wake-Up Call, Says Wada Boss," BBC, August 7, 2013.
Matt Erickson	"Georges St-Pierre on UFC Drug Testing: 'This Is Stupid,'" *USA Today*, January 15, 2014.
Katharine Gammon	"Helping Identify Performance-Enhancing Drugs, Through Chemistry," Live Science, March 19, 2014.
Nick Harris	"Born to Cheat! How World Class Athletes Can Take Drugs . . . and Get Away with It," *Daily Mail* (UK), August 24, 2013.
Independent (UK)	"Usain Bolt Says His Hair Can Be Tested for Drugs Any Time," January 12, 2014.
Brett Okamoto	"Enhanced Drug Testing Implemented," ESPN, April 29, 2014.
Press Association	"England Players to Undergo New Fifa Drug Tests at World Cup," *Guardian*, April 4, 2014.
Andrew Sharp	"The Biggest Problem with PEDs in Pro Sports," *Grantland* (blog), July 24, 2013.
Tom Verducci	"New Testing Protocols Could Change Game in Fight Against PEDs," *Sports Illustrated*, January 13, 2014.
David Wharton	"Report Names Which U.S. Athletes Faced Most Drug Testing in 2013," *Los Angeles Times*, April 2, 2014.

OPPOSING VIEWPOINTS® SERIES

Chapter 4

What Is the Future of Performance-Enhancing Drugs?

Chapter Preface

In March 2014, a team of researchers from the University of Texas at Austin made an announcement that could transform the battle against doping in sports: a test that is a thousand times more sensitive to performance-enhancing drugs (PEDs) than current ones could be coming in the near future. "How much of a drug someone took or how long ago they took it are beyond the analyst's control. The only thing you can control is how sensitive your method is," claims Daniel Armstrong, the leader of the research team. "Our goal is to develop ultra-sensitive methods that will extend the window of detection, and we have maybe the most sensitive method in the world."

The test relies on an existing technique used to detect drugs in bodily fluids known as mass spectrometry, which draws out the compounds of banned substances by mass or weight in blood, urine, or saliva. However, in a short amount of time, many PEDs are broken down to extremely low levels and are excreted, significantly narrowing the window of detection with mass spectrometry. "If the method is more sensitive, you have a longer time window to detect these substances," Armstrong explains in a March 20, 2014, article in *Chemistry World*.

To achieve significant gains in sensitivity, he and his team found a way to bring the disparate, broken-down pieces of the compounds together with paired ion electrospray ionization (PIESI). It is a process already used in laboratories to detect environmental pollutants. Armstrong reiterates that the technology is readily available and PIESI would be added as a single step to standard testing procedures. "The nice thing about it is you don't need a new instrument, it works on any electrospray mass spectrometer," he states. In the following chapter, the authors forecast the future issues, challenges, and developments of PEDs.

> *"If myostatin inhibitors do catch on as performance-enhancing drugs, they will become part of a larger trend in sports doping."*

New Muscle Drugs Could Be the Next Big Thing in Sports Doping

Jon Hamilton

In the following viewpoint, Jon Hamilton predicts that drugs blocking myostatin, the substance in the body that regulates muscle mass, could become the next big performance-enhancing drug (PED). Currently in development to treat muscular dystrophy, cancer, and other conditions, myostatin inhibitors have spurred significant muscle growth to bodybuilder proportions in mice, he says. Furthermore, the drugs are cheaper and easier than undergoing gene therapy to block myostatin, Hamilton continues, and may be undetectable after discontinuing use. Like the unexpected rise of erythropoietin (EPO) in blood doping, myostatin inhibitors could spread beyond legitimate medical use to abuse among athletes and bodybuilders, he claims. The author is a correspondent for the Science Desk at National Public Radio (NPR).

As you read, consider the following questions:

1. According to the author, how did the source of PEDs change from a decade ago?

2. Why would myostatin drugs be undetectable, as explained by Lee Sweeney?

3. What is feared if myostatin drugs become doping agents, as stated in the viewpoint?

Research intended to help people with muscle-wasting diseases could be about to launch a new era in performance-enhancing drugs.

The research has produced several muscle-building drugs now being tested in people with medical problems, including muscular dystrophy, cancer and kidney disease. The drugs all work by blocking a substance called myostatin that the body normally produces to keep muscles from getting too big.

It's likely that at least one of the drugs will receive FDA [US Food and Drug Administration] approval in the next few years, researchers say.

"When the myostatin inhibitors come along, they'll be abused," says Carlon Colker, a bodybuilder and a physician in Greenwich, Conn., who works with professional athletes. "There's no question in my mind."

One reason is that athletes and bodybuilders have seen pictures of animals like Belgian Blue bulls, which naturally lack myostatin and appear to be made of muscle. "They're huge," Colker says. "I mean they're ridiculous looking."

If myostatin inhibitors do catch on as performance-enhancing drugs, they will become part of a larger trend in sports doping. A decade ago, performance-enhancing drugs often came from rogue chemists in unregulated labs. These days, athletes are using FDA-approved products from major pharmaceutical companies.

Lance Armstrong and many other cyclists relied on the anemia drug known as EPO [erythropoietin]. Baseball players including Alex Rodriguez of the New York Yankees have been linked to another FDA-approved product, human growth hormone.

Some Muscular Mice

Athletes and bodybuilders have been fascinated by myostatin ever since it was discovered in the 1990s by a researcher at Johns Hopkins named Se-Jin Lee. If you visit Lee's mouse lab, you can see why the discovery got so much attention.

The secured facility is filled with rows of plastic cages containing some very muscular mice. "They look bulked up," he says, and they are. Lee gestures toward the cages on one shelf. "Those mice," he says, "have about twice the muscle mass of normal mice."

The mice he's talking about have been genetically engineered to lack the myostatin gene. That means their bodies don't produce the myostatin protein.

Normally, myostatin has two important roles, Lee says. In a developing embryo, it acts to limit the number of muscle fibers that are formed. Later in life, it acts to limit the growth of those muscle fibers.

"So when you get rid of the myostatin gene entirely, you see more muscle fibers, and then you get bigger muscle fibers," Lee says.

To illustrate his point, Lee sets the two plastic mouse cages on a stainless steel bench. He opens the lid of one cage and pulls out a mouse by its tail. "This mouse here is a normal male mouse about two months old," he says.

Then Lee reaches into the second cage. "Here's one of these myostatin knockout mice," he says. "I think you can appreciate how much extra muscle these mice have." It's hard to miss. The animal is not only much larger, but beneath its fur is a bodybuilder's physique.

A Stampede of Interest

At least one company devoted to bodybuilding already claims that "Genetically gifted bodybuilders have very low levels of this protein (myostatin) in their bodies, which is believed to be the cause of their muscle building gifts." Claims like this will likely cause a stampede of interest in off-label (illicit) use of anti-myostatin drugs if they come on the market. The fact that they will probably have to be injected will slow their use among teenagers, but, as the unfolding story about use of designer steroids among professional baseball players suggests, not among men and women who earn their living in competitive sports.

My guess is that use of anti-myostatin drugs will surface as an issue in professional sports within the next few years. It is even possible that a black market could emerge for anti-myostatin compounds long before a drug approved by the FDA is on the market. There is growing scientific literature on myostatin, and thousands of biochemists know how to develop antibodies.

Philip R. Reilly,
The Strongest Boy in the World:
How Genetic Information Is Reshaping Our Lives.
Cold Spring Harbor, NY: CSH Press, 2006.

Lee says he knew from the start that his discovery was going to get a lot of attention. "You only have to look at those mice for 10 seconds to realize not only the potential to treat patients, but also the potential for abuse," he says.

Athletes weren't the only ones who saw the potential for abuse. In 2008, the World Anti-Doping Agency banned substances that inhibit myostatin.

Treating Muscles That Have 'Melted Away'

If myostatin drugs do reach the market, they could help tens of thousands of patients with genetic diseases like muscular dystrophy. The drugs also might help a much larger number of people with muscle wasting associated with cancer or kidney disease or even old age.

And myostatin inhibitors could do a lot for otherwise healthy people who simply suffer an injury like a blown-out knee, says Chris Mendias, a researcher who works with orthopedic patients at the University of Michigan.

"We have to put you in a brace. You have to be non-weight-bearing for a time," he says. "The muscle will atrophy. And in a lot of cases as hard as we try, the muscle mass never comes back."

Myostatin appears to contribute to this atrophy, Mendias says. Studies show that levels of the protein rise dramatically when people stop using a particular muscle. And you can see the result in patients who have torn the knee's anterior cruciate ligament.

"It literally looks like the muscle has kind of melted away," he says. "So [we think] that if you used a myostatin inhibitor for a short period that might actually be beneficial in preventing the atrophy later on."

Another researcher with high hopes for myostatin is physiologist Lee Sweeney, who studies muscle diseases at the University of Pennsylvania. But Sweeney's optimism about new treatments is tempered by his concern about doping.

Nearly a decade ago, Sweeney wrote an article in *Scientific American* warning that myostatin manipulation could become a big problem in sports. At the time, he thought athletes might undergo gene therapy to permanently block myostatin.

Now, he says, it looks like myostatin-blocking drugs will provide a cheaper, easier and more attractive option. For one thing, Sweeney says, these products will probably leave no trace once an athlete stops taking them.

"They would have a finite sort of time that they would reside in the body and then they would be cleared," he says. "And so, unlike gene therapy, if you timed it right you might not be able to detect that they had been used."

Sweeney fears that myostatin drugs will become notorious doping agents. Then, he says, doctors may hesitate to prescribe them for legitimate uses, like helping patients with cancer or kidney disease who can no longer walk because they have lost so much muscle.

"The sort of unmet need in all these diseases far outweighs whether somebody wins a bicycle race or a sprinting event because they cheated," he says.

The Story of EPO

If the FDA does approve a myostatin inhibitor, it will probably be for a very specific group of patients. But once a drug is on the market, doctors can prescribe it to just about anyone. That's how the anemia drug EPO became such a big success after it was approved in 1989, says Jerry Avorn from Harvard Medical School.

EPO itself wasn't the problem, Avorn says.

"EPO is a wonderful drug," he says. "It does fantastic things to increase the red blood cell count and to treat anemia. And when used appropriately it's one of the best drugs that's been discovered in the last 50 years."

But no one expected this costly and potentially dangerous drug to be used by millions and millions of people, Avorn says.

"When EPO was first approved, it was approved as an orphan drug—a drug that was supposed to be used by under 200,000 people total in the U.S.," he says. "It turned out to be used by enormously greater numbers of people, partly for good reasons, partly for bad reasons."

Initially, EPO was indicated only for patients who had anemia caused by kidney failure. The FDA later added patients with anemia related to cancer chemotherapy. Then a combination of aggressive marketing and off-label prescribing helped EPO reach a whole lot of people who didn't have cancer *or* kidney disease, Avorn says.

"I've had colleagues who have had patients come to them and say, 'Doc, I saw an ad for this EPO stuff on TV last night, and I'd like you to give me some because I'd like to have a little more oomph.'"

Eventually, EPO became the most successful biotech drug in history. Global sales reached $10 billion a year despite growing evidence that high doses could cause heart problems and even death.

With so much EPO around, it's hardly surprising that some of it went to healthy athletes, Avorn says. "People—including Lance Armstrong—figured out that if you're in a bicycle race and you've got more red cells than the other people, then you will have more oxygen carrying capacity and more energy and be able to bike faster," he says.

The Future of Myostatin Drugs

So now the question is: Will drugs that inhibit myostatin become the next EPO?

"It's possible," says Colker, the physician and bodybuilder. Athletes and bodybuilders are constantly looking to medical research for the next product that will give them an edge, he says. And once a new product is widely used, people start looking for the next new thing.

The doping arms race is a bit like a cartoon, Colker says. "Daffy Duck comes out with a slingshot. And then Bugs Bunny comes back with a bat. And then Daffy Duck goes off and comes back with a gun, and then Bugs Bunny goes off and comes back with a bazooka, and then Daffy Duck goes off and comes back with an Army tank," he says. "It just keeps going and going and going."

> *"In the future, catching drug cheats ... will become more investigative with an expected rise in the use of whistleblowers and investigators with coercive powers."*

The Future of Sport: Catching Drug Cheats

Justin Robertson

Born in Australia, Justin Robertson is a digital journalist based in Toronto, Canada. He argues in the following viewpoint that testing alone will not effectively catch athletes using performance-enhancing drugs (PEDs). In fact, Robertson points out that drugs can be taken to produce negative test results for steroids. Therefore, investigations that employ tactical measures such as surveillance, compulsory testimonies, and whistleblowing will succeed in exposing drug cheats, he insists. In the future, Robertson claims, more athletes will be caught doping as the methods of testing and investigations become more sophisticated.

As you read, consider the following questions:

1. What must anti-doping organizations unearth about sports fans, as proposed by Robertson?

2. As stated by the author, what can wiretaps achieve in investigations of PEDs?

3. How can building relationships with pharmaceutical companies help doping authorities, according to the author?

Like a couple of gunslingers, Major League Baseball and Alex Rodriguez have been casting pistols at each other for the past decade, ever since the playboy third baseman became a Yankee. But like most duels, there has to be a winner and a loser. A-Rod, it seems, may have cocked his last pistol. Last week the New York native with Dominican roots was handed, by MLB, a 162-game suspension for the use of performance-enhancing drugs (PEDs). In response A-Rod is, of course, suing everyone. He's suing the players' union for their lack of support. He's also suing the league because he thinks they are out to "get him," which they are because he f----- up. ESPN's legal analyst Roger Cossack said it best: "He [A-Rod] believes Major League Baseball is out to get him. And, you know, in some ways he's not being paranoid because Major League Baseball is out to get him. Just like cops are out to get bank robbers, they believe he broke the rules and they *were* out to get him." Once the legal hoopla is dust, A-Rod will most likely serve his 162-game holiday which means Major League Baseball won the duel. They got their man.

Sport has evolved into a finely tuned business. It's no longer simply organized athletics. Across many codes of sport, not just baseball, whether athletes or teams are taking performance-enhancing drugs to help make them stronger or using them to help them recover faster, modern-day professional sport has become more of a science than we know—drugs have become an integral part of it. The mantra of "win at all costs" trumps fair play. And now, there is this notion that sports science is an essential ingredient to success. Push harder, smash records, recover faster. With world anti-doping organizations at the helm left to figure out the future methods of advanced blood testing and eradicating cheats from sport, they must unearth what fans really want from sport: clean sports with high morals and values (and possibly lower quality of athletes) or the best athletes performing at their peak every time they take the field injected with performance-enhancing drugs? As it stands, athletes—as Lance Armstrong eluded to in his "come clean" interview with Oprah—don't see the point in playing clean when everyone else is playing dirty.

This time last year on the other side of the world, Australian political ministers, heads of sport and crime chiefs stood around a rickety wooden lectern. They each took their turn at barking their disgust at a 12-month long investigation conducted by the Australian Crime Commission (A.C.C) that revealed its sporting heroes, across multiple codes of sport, were believed to be taking illegal performance-enhancing drugs. It was dubbed the "blackest day" in the history of Australian sport, an $8.82 billion dollar industry. The report revealed an increase of 255 per cent between 2009 and 2011 in the number of hormones detected at the Australian border by the Australian Customs and Border Protection Service. The commission drew parallels to the doping program involving Lance Armstrong and his team mates. "The difference is, the Australian threat is current, crosses more than one sporting code and is evolving" the report states.

When the A.C.C disclosed to the media their threats of "if you cheat, you will be caught" in February, they also highlighted some of their covert methods for catching these alleged drug cheats: wiretaps. As it stands, the powers of the A.C.C allows them to conduct wiretaps but the information retrieved cannot be shared or used as evidence and only acts as a stepping stone where they can then interrogate and question potential law breakers. What wiretaps achieve, potentially, is a lead to suppliers, users to learn more about the types of drugs athletes are using. It's the type of information regulatory blood testing can't retrieve.

Montreal's World Anti-Doping Agency (WADA) says, to beat drug cheats in sport, investigations will need to be deployed in an increased effort to nab illegal drug users according to their "Coordinating Investigations and Sharing Anti-Doping Information and Evidence" report. The focus for WADA is to build partnerships between sports movements and public authorities that will allow anti-doping organizations to search and seize, survey, and legally conduct compulsory witness testimonies under penalties of perjury. Where blood testing fails, surveillance and underground investigations excel. These tactical measures could force a testimonial (e.g., Lance Armstrong). One bit of information could unravel a long string of unethical drugging methods in sport and ideally shut down suppliers, pharmacists and backyard drug-mixing dens. The war on drugs will not be won through regular drug testing in laboratories. Sport must now shift to a new paradigm. In the future, catching drug cheats will involve not only blood tests, but will become more investigative with an expected rise in the use of whistleblowers and investigators with coercive powers.

More recently there have been calls for "blood passports" in tennis, which would measure the history of an athlete's levels of substances over a period of time. Good for the long term, not so for the short term. As former drug supplier to Marion Jones, Angel Heredia said in an interview with *Spiegel* magazine, there are drugs that can hide everything. For example, there are tablets you can take for the kidneys that block the metabolites of steroids and thus test negative and there are also chemicals you can digest hours before a race that prevent acidification in the muscles, making it undetectable for doping testers. Heredia said the future of catching more drug cheats lies in a universal system and regular testing: "If all federations and sponsors and managers and athletes and trainers were all in agreement, if they were to invest all the money that the sport generates and if every athlete were to be tested twice a week—only then (could sport become clean)." But neither methods are quick and both are costly. Some experts say building relationships with pharmaceutical companies so they know ahead of time what the latest drugs on the market are and can plan testing around that intel.

It's sad that sport has come to this, this state of artificially becoming great or being pro instead of training hard, practicing long into the night and doing it commonly and instinctively. More and more athletes will get caught in 2014 by league investigations because cheats eventually lose and methods of catching cheats will be more sophisticated. But will that stop the common pro athlete from trying to find "the edge" to whip his rival? Most likely no. We have this maudlin perception of sport that our athletes must be pure and flawless and role models for our kids. We often forget their perspective: It's their job to perform at the highest caliber possible to win. Athletes want to taste victory and will do anything to reach that objective. "Win at all costs," they say. We forget too, ever since sport has existed athletes have always searched for that extra edge, whether it be injecting performance drugs or sipping magic potions. The culture will never change. We've never known sport without PEDs. Sport almost depends on PEDs now. Could you imagine if, starting now, every athlete stopped taking PEDs? Now imagine the performances. Also think about all the records created through time by beefed up athletes and how those records will never ever be broken. As fans, we like seeing records broken. It's like cheering on the underdog.

The message from the MLB to A-rod was based on the perception of taking drugs: It doesn't set a good example for the kids and it doesn't look good for baseball's image. In the future of sport, every code will have their own way of tackling drug cheats. Some codes will rely heavily on a rival's confession; some will turn a blind eye until they have to do something about it. Major League Baseball is the sheriff of North America and guard their precious game with loaded guns and a swiveling toothpick in their mouth. They are on the hunt for drug-swilling rats. Consider this: When you try to accost the wily sheriff at sundown, you better wear a tin-proof vest because it doesn't matter how big a superstar you are—I'm looking at you A-Rod—if you fight the law, the law will win.

> "With unemployment among graduates at record levels, more and more students are turning to 'cognitive enhancing drugs.'"

The Dangers for Students Addicted to Brain Viagra

Steve Bird

In the following viewpoint, Steve Bird writes that "cognitive enhancing drugs" or "smart drugs" are gaining popularity among students. Bird states that drugs, like Modafinil, allow users to enhance their focus, thus earning them higher grades. Also, he maintains that obtaining these drugs can be cheap and easy, thanks to modern technology. However, the author warns, there are risks involved with drugs such as these. Impacts can range from physical (vomiting and tremors) to social (withdrawing from friends and family), Bird reports. The author offers a student perspective about what it is like to use smart drugs. Bird is a reporter for the Daily Mail.

As you read, consider the following questions:

1. According to the author, what do students hope to gain from using "cognitive enhancing drugs"?

2. What are the near-term benefits of using Modafinil pills, stated by the author? What are the side effects?

3. What, in the author's opinion, makes obtaining smart drugs easy?

Drugs Claimed to Boost Your Intellect Are Sweeping Universities—But at What Cost?

Generations of students have depended on nothing more potent than gallons of black coffee to enable them to burn the midnight oil when studying. But now a far more sinister stimulant is sweeping campuses.

With unemployment among graduates at record levels, more and more students are turning to 'cognitive enhancing drugs' in the hope of boosting their grades and therefore their job prospects.

The most popular of these drugs is Modafinil, a prescription-only stimulant used by doctors to treat patients suffering from the sleeping disorder narcolepsy.

Indeed, a new inquiry suggests that up to a quarter of students at some leading universities have experimented with it.

As a result, a highly profitable black market has developed in this and other prescription-only medicines designed to treat acute neurological conditions.

Modafinil pills are being sold for as little as 50p each and have been proven to improve memory by 10 per cent. They keep users alert and awake, increasing their ability to concentrate and process information.

However, they can have worrying side effects—including headaches, irritableness, vomiting, irrational behaviour, tremors, palpitations and broken sleeping patterns.

Yet an investigation by the *Mail* has found the pills are widely available online. Websites based in Asia and the Far East, as well as British 'smart drug entrepreneurs', peddle them to students, academics and even city workers desperate to get an apparent 'edge' over their rivals.

The drug is being carefully marketed to suggest that it can unlock hidden human potential.

One website, being run from Turkey, uses a picture of the actor Bradley Cooper in the Hollywood film *Limitless*—Cooper plays a character who becomes almost super-human after taking a pill that unleashes 100 per cent of his brain power.

It took just minutes of trawling the Internet for the *Mail* to be able to buy Modafinil for just 50p a pill from a Hong Kong website. Ten stronger tablets were also purchased for just £17 from a man in Dorset who posted his email address on student Internet forums and offered to sell the drug. They all arrived within a week.

If they are this easy to obtain, how many aspiring students are succumbing to the temptation to take so-called 'smart pills'?

In a recent inquiry by Sky News, one student at Oxford claimed up to one in four students had taken Modafinil.

A survey by *Varsity*, the University of Cambridge paper, found that 10 per cent of students there admitted taking Modafinil or drugs like it to improve their ability to concentrate.

So exactly what are the dangers of using Modafinil in this way? More importantly, how can parents spot the signs that their children are using it?

One 24-year-old former student we spoke to—who we will call James—said smart pills were a regular part of his and his friends' study routine while he read politics at Cambridge University. The drug was so popular, he says, that stickers were even put up around the library by students selling Modafinil.

'It gave you that edge. You had a sort of study tunnel vision and your brain worked more like a computer as it processed information,' he says. 'It was an aid for taking notes out of books and revision when you need to just churn through stuff.

Cognitive Enhancement and Equality

If you're thinking about something like surgical procedures for implanting genetically engineered tissue into someone's brain, or if you're talking about very high tech brain-to-computer interfacing technologies or the genetic engineering of human embryos, presumably those technologies are going to be very expensive and won't be available to a lot of people. So if that's the direction that we go, there might be very serious problems of inequality.

On the other hand cognitive enhancements like TDCS [transcranial direct-current stimulation] and cognition-enhancing drugs may become inexpensive fairly quickly, and in turn might diffuse much more rapidly than literacy did. This is especially clear in the context of prescription drugs. Right now if you go to Wal-Mart there are over one hundred and thirty drugs that used to be on patent and have now gone off patent and gone generic, and a month supply of each of these drugs is only four dollars. Now that's a lot cheaper than the cognitive enhancement drug that you get at Starbucks. So yes in the future there might be a period when these drugs are on patent, and are expensive, but when they go off patent they could become very inexpensive.

Allen Buchanan as told to Ross Andersen,
"Why Cognitive Enhancement Is in Your Future
(and Your Past)," Atlantic, February 6, 2012.

'You could go 12 hours without looking up from your books—you were totally focused.'

From his second year, James began buying Modafinil from 'pharmaceutical websites' based in the Far East or Asia, the same sort that bombard inboxes with adverts for Viagra.

In his final year he took it solidly for a month.

Within minutes of taking one of these small, white, chalky pills, the heart rate begins to quicken. As the drug starts to really take effect, the user feels more energetic and focused.

'I would get up at 8am, pop a 100mg pill and go back to sleep,' says James. 'Half an hour later, when the pill kicked in, you would wake up feeling very alert. It would begin to wear off by about 6pm.

'Some of my friends were taking 400mg a day. There was a big difference between the branded pill and the inferior ones from spurious websites.

'The cheaper ones made you buzz as your heart raced a bit. There was no way of knowing what was really in the pills.'

After regular use, he increased his dosage to 200mg a day. But James, who spoke on the condition of anonymity, began to notice worrying side effects.

'I thought it was a bit like taking Pro-Plus (over-the-counter caffeine pills) or drinking strong coffee. But, it wasn't. You wouldn't take it to help with creativity. And you certainly wouldn't have one before an exam, in part because you constantly need the toilet.

'After popping one, I wouldn't want any social interaction, which was useful because no one could tempt you away from studying with the offer of going to the pub for a pint. Sometimes I wouldn't eat for the entire day. It felt like my energy was coming from the pill itself.

'It did have an effect on my relationships because my girlfriend noticed a difference in my behaviour. I had mood swings and was quite irritable. It was as if I didn't like being around people. We had quite a lot of arguments. It also destroyed much of my social life.'

James, who graduated with a 2:1 three years ago, won't take Modafinil any more because he fears it could have long-term effects on his brain, mood and relationships.

While it is not illegal to possess or buy Modafinil, anyone in the UK selling it on the black market faces up to two years in jail. The drug works by improving the efficiency of neurotransmitters, the chemicals that relay signals between cells in the brain.

Ilina Singh, professor of science, ethics and society at King's College London, says that there is very little reliable evidence about Modafinil use in the UK, but suggests that probably 'around 10 per cent' of students have used it at least once. In the U.S. around 16 per cent of the student population is said to be using smart drugs.

Professor Barbara Sahakian, a neuroscientist at Cambridge University, is concerned that very little is known about the long-term effects of Modafinil. 'Students feel pressure is being put on them to take drugs like Modafinil because they believe other students are taking them. If they don't take them, they think they will be at a disadvantage,' she says.

'Not enough research has been done to see what effects these have on fit and healthy people.'

What is worryingly evident is that Internet forums about smart drugs, also called nootropics—derived from the Greek for 'mind' and 'bend' or 'turn'—are buzzing with people discussing the best ways to buy them.

Students trade email addresses and mobile phone numbers of dealers, as well as pharmacy websites abroad that have proven trustworthy. They give testimonials claiming that Modafinil—occasionally called 'Viagra for the brain'—helped them plough through reading lists or cram for their exams.

Others note how the drug made them feel 'tired, yet awake', 'buzzy' or gave them a headache, stopped them sleeping or made their heart race.

This year alone, 9,610 illegal websites around the world selling counterfeit and unlicensed medicines have been closed down. In just one week this summer, the Medicines and Healthcare Products Regulatory Agency seized £12.2 million of unlicensed drugs in the UK, including Modafinil, Viagra and the attention deficit disorder drug Ritalin.

Experts warn would-be buyers that there is no way of being sure they are getting the authentic drug from the black market or from abroad. Research has shown that some pills are at best sugar-coated placebos, and at worst toxic.

The pack from Hong Kong that the *Mail* received arrived in a brown padded envelope. It was marked as containing a 'healthcare product'. Inside was a single blister pack of ten pills, each 100mg, labelled Modalert.

Remarkably, the company that sold them, United Pharmacies, is not breaking any laws because it is legal to sell Modafinil in the region where it is based.

It states: 'A prescription is not required as we are an Oceania-based company and operate under different laws and regulations.'

However, it has clearly identified a market for Modafinil, which it describes as a 'study drug', in Britain. United Pharmacies prices its pills in sterling, has an English website and has a London-based telephone number which connects to a man in Hong Kong who speaks with a refined English accent.

The website does advise customers to consult a doctor and warns of the drug's possible side effects including nausea, headaches, diarrhoea, tremors, nervousness, confusion, insomnia, palpitations and unusual behaviour.

Then there are the UK-based 'smart drug' entrepreneurs who sell Modafinil to cash-strapped students worried about being defrauded if they buy from abroad.

They offer pills at nearly £2 a tablet—nearly three or four times the price on offshore websites. Mike, a dealer from Poole, explained in an email that in a good week he can sell 20 packs of the stronger 200mg pills at £17 each, making him at least a few hundred pounds tax free. He bulk-buys from an Internet pharmaceutical company.

Like others, Mike posts his email address or mobile phone number in the comments sections of forums. In this black market consultancy, no medical questions are asked and no health advice is offered.

In the meantime, students may be boosting their exam grades—but at what cost to their health, only time will tell.

In a statement, a spokesman for Universities UK, an organisation representing university vice-chancellors, said: 'We would be very concerned if the impression were given that most students at UK universities are now taking 'smart drugs'.

'We are not aware of any new research or data to suggest that such drugs are widely used and available among the UK's higher education student population of 2.5 million students.

'Discussions on this topic in the past have been based largely on anecdotal evidence or on surveys conducted in the United States.'

| *"There is plenty of evidence that cognitive enhancement is cheating."*

The Use of Cognitive-Enhancing Drugs Is Cheating and Problematic

George Dawson

In the following viewpoint, George Dawson asserts that using drugs for cognitive performance is cheating and dangerous. Focusing on attention deficit hyperactivity disorder (ADHD) medications taken to boost alertness and concentration, Dawson disputes the view that such stimulants do not improve academic performance, giving users an unfair edge. Additionally, he argues that permitting the use of stimulants as cognitive enhancers ignores their addictive properties and health hazards. Dawson continues that stimulants can actually cause ADHD-like symptoms, especially among college students, who are most likely to experiment and abuse drugs. Based in Minnesota, Dawson is a psychiatrist and blogger for Real Psychiatry, *which addresses issues in the field's practice and research.*

As you read, consider the following questions:

1. How does Dawson respond to the view that it is possible to improve concentration and not improve learning?

2. How does the author address the argument that using performance-enhancing drugs (PEDs) in sports is cheating, but cognitive enhancement is not?

3. What in-depth experience does society have with stimulants, as stated by Dawson?

One of my colleagues posted a recent commentary from *Nature* on how the idea of the smart pill has been oversold. The basic theme of the commentary is that there is no good evidence that treatment of ADHD [attention deficit hyperactivity disorder] with stimulants improves academic outcomes. The author reviews a few long-term studies and contends that differences between the medication and placebo seem to wash out over time and therefore there is no detectable difference. Her overall conclusions seem inconsistent with her view that "[f]or most people with ADHD, these medications—typically formulations of methylphenidate or amphetamine—quickly calm them down and increase their ability to concentrate. Although these behavioural changes make the drugs useful, a growing body of evidence suggests that the benefits mainly stop there. . . ."

Not Enhanced Performance?

A question for any cognitive psychologists out there—is it possible to improve your concentration and have that not improve learning? I can't imagine how that happens. If you go from not being able to read 2 pages at a time to suddenly reading chapters at a time, how is that not enhanced cognitive performance? If you go from staring out the window all day and daydreaming to being able to focus on what the teacher is saying, how will that not lead to an improved outcome? The idea that improved attention—a central factor in human cognition—will not affect anything over time suggests to me that the measures being used for follow up are not very robust or that this is a skewed sample of opinion.

For the purpose of cognitive enhancement, the typical users are students trying to gain an edge by increasing their study time. Anyone who has experienced college and professional school realizes that there is a large amount of information to be mastered, and it is not presented in an efficient way. I can never recall a professor who advised us of the important guideposts along the way or gave us any shortcuts. The usual message is study all of this material in depth every day, or you will fall behind. That approach in general is consistent with gaps in the ability to study either through the normal course of life or the competition for intellectual resources by 3 or 4 other professors who regard their courses as important. That typically results in a pattern of cramming for specific key exams. Although I have not seen any specific studies, stimulant medications are generally used for this purpose, and, in many cases, the use is widespread. There is a literature on the number of college students who may be feigning ADHD symptoms in order to get a prescription and that number could be as high as 50%.

Stimulants as a Smart Pill

What about the issue of stimulants acting as a smart pill in people who don't have ADHD? In the most comprehensive review I could find on the subject, the authors review laboratory studies and conclude that in those settings stimulants enhance consolidation of declarative learning to varying degrees, had mixed effects on working memory, and mixed effects on cognitive control. On 8 additional tests of executive function, the authors found that stimulant medication enhance performance on two of those tests—non-verbal fluency and non-verbal intelligence. They have the interesting observation that small effects could be important in a competitive environment. Their review also provides an excellent overview of the epidemiology of stimulant use on campuses that suggests that the overall prevalence is high and the pattern of use is consistent with cramming for exams. They cite a reference that I could not find that was a re-analysis of NSDUH [National Survey on Drug Use and Health] data suggesting that as many as 1 in 20 stimulant users may have a problem with excessive use and dependence.

Getting back to the theme of the *Nature* commentary, it is ironic that the smart pill theme is being called into question when it was the subject of a *Nature* article years earlier advocating for the use of cognitive enhancement. In that article, [researcher H.] Greely et al. come to the somewhat astounding conclusion:

"Based on our consideration, we call for a presumption that mentally competent adults should be able to engage in cognitive enhancement using drugs."

They arrive at that conclusion by rejecting three arguments against this practice. Those arguments include that it is cheating, it is not natural, and it is drug abuse. Their rejection of the cheating argument is interesting because they accept the idea that performance-enhancing drugs (PEDs) in sports is cheating. They reject that in cognitive enhancement claiming that there would need to be a set of rules outlining what forms of enhancement would be outlawed and what would not (e.g., drugs versus tutors). To me that seems like a stretch. I think that sports bodies select performance-enhancing drugs as a specific target because it clearly alters body physiology in a way that cannot be altered by any other means. There is also plenty of evidence that the types of PEDs are dangerous to the health of athletes and associated with deaths. Their conclusion about drug abuse: "But drugs are regulated on a scale that subjectively judges the potential for harm from the very dangerous (heroin) to the relatively harmless (caffeine). Given such regulation, the mere fact that cognitive enhancers are drugs is no reason to outlaw them." That is a serious misread of the potential addictive properties of stimulants and the previous epidemics that occurred when the drugs were FDA [US Food and Drug Administration] approved for weight loss, the epidemic of street use in the 1970s, and the current and ongoing epidemic of meth labs and methamphetamine use throughout much of the USA.

Highly Problematic Goals

These authors go on to outline four policy mechanisms that they believe would "support fairness, protect individuals from coercion, and minimize enhancement related socioeconomic disparities." At first glance, these lofty goals might seem reasonable if society had not already had in-depth experience with the drugs in question. The clearest example was the FDA approved indication of amphetamines for weight loss. What could be a more equitable application than providing amphetamines to any American who wanted to use them for weight loss? The resulting epidemic and reversal of the FDA decision is history. A similarly equitable decision to liberalize opioids in the treatment of chronic pain had resulted in another epidemic of higher lethality due to differences in the toxicology of opioids and amphetamines.

The contrast between these two commentaries in *Nature* also highlight a couple of the issues about the way medical problems and treatment is portrayed in the media. This first is that you can't have it both ways. Quoting a researcher or two out of context does not constitute an accurate assessment of the science involved. Some of the authors in the first commentary are highly respected researchers in cognitive science and they clearly believe that cognitive enhancement occurs, and it should be widely applied. *Nature* or any other journal cannot have it both ways. . . . The second issue is that in both cases the authors seem blind to the addictive properties of stimulants, and they are ignorant of what happens when there is more access as exemplified by the FDA misstep of approving stimulants for weight loss. Do we really need a new epidemic to demonstrate this phenomenon again? Thirdly, all of this comes paying lip service to non-medication strategies for cognitive enhancement. We can talk about the importance of adequate sleep—a known cause of ADHD-like symptoms—and if we are running universities and workplaces in a manner that creates sleep-deprived states, the next step is reaching for pills to balance an unbalanced lifestyle. The new rules for residency training are a better step in the right direction. Fourth, college is a peak time for alcohol and substance use in the lives of most Americans. These substances in general can lead to a syndrome that looks like ADHD. It is highly problematic to make that diagnosis and provide a medication that can be used in an addictive manner. It is also highly problematic to think that treating an addicted person with a stimulant will cure them of the addiction, and yet it happens all of the time.

Old Drugs with Bad Side Effects

There is plenty of evidence to suggest that cognitive enhancement is cheating. Much of my career has been spent correcting the American tendency of trying to balance one medication against another and using medications to tolerate a toxic lifestyle or workplace. It does not work, and the current group of medications that are being put forward as cognitive enhancers are generally old drugs with bad side effect profiles, particularly with respect to the potential for addiction.

If you want safe cognitive enhancers that can be made widely available, they have not been invented yet.

Periodical and Internet Sources Bibliography

The following articles have been selected to supplement the diverse views presented in this chapter.

American Chemical Society — "New Method Is a Thousand Times More Sensitive to Performance-Enhancing Drugs," March 18, 2014.

Ross Andersen — "Why Cognitive Enhancement Is in Your Future (and Your Past)," *Atlantic*, February 6, 2012.

Mitchell Culler — "Drugs Should Be Considered Cheating," *Daily Collegian* (Penn State University), February 17, 2014.

Jonathan Gatehouse — "The Athlete Whisperer: Wayne Halliwell Teaches Mental Strategies That Land Olympians on the Podium," *Maclean's*, March 3, 2014.

James L. Kent — "Adderall: America's Favorite Amphetamine," *Huffington Post*, October 29, 2013.

Terry Newell — "Lance Armstrong and the Future of Performance Enhancement," *Huffington Post*, August 31, 2012.

Emma Stoye — "Super Sensitive Test Hones In on Performance Enhancing Drugs," Chemistry World, March 20, 2014.

Maia Szalavitz — "Performance-Enhancing Drugs O.K. in School, but Not in Sports, Students Say," *Time*, May 9, 2012.

Helen Thompson — "Performance Enchantment: Superhuman Athletes," *Nature*, July 19, 2012.

David Wood — "The Coming Revolution in Mental Enhancement," *H+*, March 12, 2013.

For Further Discussion

Chapter 1

1. Michael Rosenberg claims that performance-enhancing drugs are damaging to professional sports. What reasons does Rosenberg cite for making this argument? Do you agree with Rosenberg's argument? Why, or why not?

2. Leigh Cowart argues that athletes should not be allowed to use performance-enhancing drugs solely because they are genetically inferior to their opponents. In your opinion, does Cowart provide sufficient evidence to support her conclusion? Explain your reasoning.

Chapter 2

1. Chris Doorley reports on the life-threatening side effects of performance-enhancing drugs. What are some examples of these side effects? Why do you think some athletes put themselves at risk and take performance-enhancing drugs despite these dangerous side effects? Explain.

2. David Crary argues that human growth hormone use has increased among teenagers and that the drug is dangerous and largely unregulated. Conversely, Kent Sepkowitz claims that the hormone does not have serious side effects. Which author offers the more compelling argument, and why?

Chapter 3

1. John J. Ross contends that testing for performance-enhancing drugs has its limitations. What evidence does Ross provide that leads him to this conclusion? Do you agree with Ross's argument? Why, or why not?

2. Blair Henley argues that a biological passport system for detecting performance-enhancing drugs in the sport of

tennis would be ineffective. Based on the information in the viewpoint, do you agree with Henley? Why, or why not?

Chapter 4

1. According to Justin Robertson, more and more professional athletes would get caught using performance-enhancing drugs if leagues would carry out investigations. Does Robertson offer compelling evidence to support his argument? Explain your answer.

2. Steve Bird argues that cognitive-enhancing drugs are gaining popularity among students. He says these drugs allow students to enhance their focus to earn good grades. What are some of the side effects associated with these drugs that Bird mentions? Do you think using "smart drugs" is cheating, as argued by George Dawson? Explain your reasoning.

Organizations to Contact

The editors have compiled the following list of organizations concerned with the issues debated in this book. The descriptions are derived from materials provided by the organizations. All have publications or information available for interested readers. The list was compiled on the date of publication of the present volume; the information provided here may change. Be aware that many organizations take several weeks or longer to respond to inquiries, so allow as much time as possible.

Anti-Doping Sciences Institute (ADSI)
(800) 920-6605
e-mail: info@antidopingsciences.org
website: www.antidopingsciences.org

The Anti-Doping Sciences Institute (ADSI) is a provider of analytical testing and consulting services related to performance-enhancing drug use in sports. ADSI provides an array of services, including designing and conducting drug testing programs, performing supplement testing and analysis, offering expert consulting to sports organizations, and managing information hotlines for competitors. ADSI's website offers information about its services as well as a link to the founder's blog, which features articles such as "Athletes, Drug Testing, and Deer Antler—The Real Story."

Association Against Steroid Abuse (AASA)
521 N. Sam Houston Parkway E, Suite 635
Houston, TX   77060
website: www.steroidabuse.com

The Association Against Steroid Abuse (AASA) is an educational organization that provides information and statistics on the dangers and issues of anabolic steroid abuse. Its website includes information about different steroids, steroid abuse, steroids and sports, the law, steroid myths, and steroids and women. Additionally, its website offers an Ask the Doctor section that features frequently asked questions and answers about many different aspects of steroid use and abuse.

International Association of Athletics Federations (IAAF)

17 rue Princesse Florestine, BP359, Monaco Cedex MC 98007
+377 93 10 88 88 • fax: +377 93 15 95 15
website: www.iaaf.org/home

The International Association of Athletics Federations (IAAF) is the international governing body of track-and-field athletics. The IAAF is committed to keeping its athletes healthy and in compliance with its zero-tolerance policy with respect to doping. The association has several departments, including the Medical and Anti-Doping Department, and its website offers an anti-doping section for athletes. Among IAAF's many publications are the *IAAF Anti-Doping Regulations* and the *IAAF News* newsletter.

National Center for Drug Free Sport

2537 Madison Avenue, Kansas City, MO 64108
(816) 474-8655 • fax: (816) 502-9287
website: www.drugfreesport.com

The National Center for Drug Free Sport administers drug tests required by the National Collegiate Athletic Association (NCAA). It also provides drug-use prevention services to athletic organizations. Through its subscription-based Resource Exchange Center, the organization offers updated information on banned substances and drug testing procedures.

National Institute on Drug Abuse (NIDA)

6001 Executive Boulevard, Room 5213
MSC 9561 Bethesda, MD 20892-9561
(301) 443-1124
website: www.drugabuse.gov

The National Institute on Drug Abuse (NIDA) is part of the National Institutes of Health (NIH), a component of the United States Department of Health and Human Services.

NIDA supports and conducts research on drug abuse—including the yearly Monitoring the Future survey—to improve addiction prevention, treatment, and policy efforts. It publishes the bimonthly *NIDA Notes* newsletter along with public education materials, including the research report "Anabolic Steroid Abuse" and the drug fact sheet "Anabolic Steroids."

National Strength and Conditioning Association (NSCA)
1885 Bob Johnson Drive, Colorado Springs, CO   80906
(800) 815-6826 • fax: (719) 632-6367
e-mail: nsca@nsca.com
website: www.nsca.com/Home

The National Strength and Conditioning Association (NSCA) brings together strength and sports coaches, sports scientists, researchers, educators, physical therapists, physicians, athletic trainers, and personal trainers. The association provides educational resources and opportunities for its members and strives to develop and promote the profession of strength training and conditioning. Among its publications are the *Strength and Conditioning Journal* and the *Personal Training Quarterly*.

Office of National Drug Control Policy (ONDCP)
The White House, 1600 Pennsylvania Avenue NW
Washington, DC   20500
(202) 456-1111
e-mail: oipl@ondcp.eop.gov
website: www.whitehouse.gov/ondcp

The Office of National Drug Control Policy (ONDCP) develops and coordinates public health strategies to fight drug abuse and address the economic, political, social, and health concerns related to drug abuse. It also focuses on a "renewed emphasis on community-based prevention programs, early intervention programs in healthcare settings, . . . funding scientific research on drug use, and . . . expanding access to substance abuse treatment." The ONDCP publishes the president's National Drug Control Strategy, an annual report on the nation's approach to drug policy. The agency's website features the ONDCP blog, which provides updates on drug policy and articles such as "Springtime: A Good Time to Think About Our Kids and Steroids."

SteroidLaw.com

e-mail: info@cmgesq.com
website: www.steroidlaw.com

Run by criminal attorney and former bodybuilder Rick Collins, SteroidLaw.com is a website that provides health and legal information regarding the use of steroids. The website espouses that the health risks of steroids have been exaggerated and advocates for the reform of current steroid laws. Numerous resources are available on the website, including the article "Beyond the High Profile Steroids Cases: Not Every Case Is as High Profile as Alex Rodriguez, but Everyone May Have Just as Much to Lose."

Substance Abuse and Mental Health Services Administration (SAMHSA)

1 Choke Cherry Road, Rockville, MD   20857
(877) 726-4727
website: www.samhsa.gov

The Substance Abuse and Mental Health Services Administration (SAMHSA) is an agency within the United States Department of Health and Human Services that seeks to reduce the impact of substance abuse and mental illness in the United States. SAMHSA provides reports, fact sheets, and videos on steroid abuse, prevention, and treatment. Some of the publications available on the SAMHSA website include "Anabolic Steroid Abuse" and "Tips for Teens: The Truth About Steroids."

United States Anti-Doping Agency (USADA)

5555 Tech Center Drive, Suite 200
Colorado Springs, CO   80919
(866) 601-2632 • fax: (719) 785-2001

e-mail: media@usada.org
website: www.usada.org

The United States Anti-Doping Agency (USADA) manages the drug testing of US Olympic, Paralympic, Pan American, and Parapan American athletes and enforces sanctions against athletes who violate drug laws. The agency promotes educational programs to inform athletes of the rules governing the use of performance-enhancing drugs, the ethics of doping, and doping's harmful effects. *The Spirit of Sport* newsletter is available on USADA's website.

United States Drug Enforcement Administration (DEA)

8701 Morrissette Drive, Springfield, VA   22152
(202) 307-1000
website: www.justice.gov/dea/index.shtml

The United States Drug Enforcement Administration (DEA) is a division within the US Department of Justice that focuses on enforcing the nation's drug laws and reducing the amount of illegal drugs available to consumers in the United States. The DEA investigates and prosecutes drug gangs and smugglers; collaborates with legislators and policy makers to formulate an effective and comprehensive drug policy; and coordinates with other countries and international organizations to confront international drug smuggling. The DEA is responsible for enforcing prescription drug laws and determining the federal approach to fighting prescription drug abuse. The DEA website provides several resources, including a drug fact sheet about the dangers of steroid abuse.

World Anti-Doping Agency (WADA)

800 Place Victoria, Suite 1700, PO Box 120
Montreal, Quebec   H4Z 1B7
   Canada
+1 514 904 9232 • fax: +1 514 904 8650
website: www.wada-ama.org

The World Anti-Doping Agency (WADA) was created in 1999 as an independent international anti-doping agency. The agency works with international sports federations, national and international Olympic committees, governments, and athletes to coordinate a comprehensive drug testing program. WADA has begun conducting unannounced, out-of-competition tests that it believes will reduce the prevalence of drugs in the Olympics and other international competitions. Its website offers publications such as the magazine *Play True* and the leaflet "Dangers of Doping."

Bibliography of Books

Reed Albergotti and Vanessa O'Connell
Wheelmen: Lance Armstrong, the Tour de France, and the Greatest Sports Conspiracy Ever. New York: Penguin, 2013.

Shaun Assael
Steroid Nation: Juiced Home Run Totals, Anti-Aging Miracles, and a Hercules in Every High School: The Secret History of America's True Drug Addiction. New York: ESPN, 2008.

Rob Beamish
Steroids: A New Look at Performance-Enhancing Drugs. Santa Barbara, CA: Praeger, 2011.

Michael A. Bonventre
Drug Testing Exposed Loopholes and Trade Secrets: How Businesses, Federal & State Agencies, Law Enforcement, Users & Rehabilitation Profit from Them. Seattle, WA: CreateSpace, 2011.

Allen Buchanan
Better than Human: The Promise and Perils of Enhancing Ourselves. New York: Oxford University Press, 2011.

Chris Cooper
Run, Swim, Throw, Cheat: The Science Behind Drugs in Sport. New York: Oxford University Press, 2012.

Tim Elfrink and Gus Garcia-Roberts
Blood Sport: Alex Rodriguez, Biogenesis, and the Quest to End Baseball's Steroid Era. New York: Penguin, 2014.

David Epstein — *The Sports Gene: Inside the Science of Extraordinary Athletic Performance.* New York: Penguin, 2013.

Jean L. Fourcroy, ed. — *Pharmacology, Doping and Sports: A Scientific Guide for Athletes, Coaches, Physicians, Scientists and Administrators.* New York: Routledge, 2008.

Jeri Freedman — *Steroids: High-Risk Performance Drugs.* New York: Rosen, 2009.

Katrin Gerlinger, Thomas Petermann, and Arnold Sauter — *Gene Doping: Scientific Basis—Gateways—Monitoring.* Berlin, Germany: Office of Technology Assessment at the German Bundestag, 2013.

Carl Germano — *The Misled Athlete: Effective Nutritional and Training Strategies Without the Need for Steroids, Stimulants and Banned Substances.* Bloomington, IN: iUniverse, 2011.

Tyler Hamilton and Daniel Coyle — *The Secret Race: Inside the Hidden World of the Tour de France.* New York: Bantam, 2013.

Elisabeth Hildt and Andreas G. Franke, eds. — *Cognitive Enhancement: An Interdisciplinary Perspective.* New York: Springer, 2013.

Doug Kirk — *The Spin: What's the Future of Cycling and Performance-Enhancing Drugs?* Denver, CO: Outskirt Press, 2013.

Will Leitch — *God Save the Fan: How Steroid Hypocrites, Soul-Sucking Suits, and a Worldwide Leader Not Named Bush Have Taken the Fun Out of Sports.* New York: HarperCollins, 2009.

Maxwell J. Mehlman — *The Price of Perfection: Individualism and Society in the Era of Biomedical Enhancement.* Baltimore, MD: Johns Hopkins University Press, 2009.

Elaine A. Moore — *The Amphetamine Debate: The Use of Adderall, Ritalin and Related Drugs for Behavior Modification, Neuroenhancement and Anti-Aging Purposes.* Jefferson, NC: McFarland, 2010.

David R. Mottram, ed. — *Drugs in Sport.* 5th ed. New York: Routledge, 2010.

Stephen Mumford — *Watching Sport: Aesthetics, Ethics and Emotion.* New York: Routledge, 2011.

Jim Parry, Mark Nesti, and Nick Watson, eds. — *Theology, Ethics and Transcendence in Sports.* New York: Routledge, 2010.

Kirk Radomski — *Bases Loaded: The Inside Story of the Steroid Era in Baseball by the Central Figure in the Mitchell Report.* New York: Hudson Street Press, 2009.

Alex Simpson — *Chemically Engineered: The Science of Steroids and Muscle.* Seattle, WA: CreateSpace, 2014.

Bob Stewart and Aaron Smith
Rethinking Drug Use in Sport: Why the War Will Never Be Won. New York: Routledge, 2014.

Mario Thevis
Mass Spectrometry in Sports Drug Testing: Characterization of Prohibited Substances and Doping Control Analytical Assays. New York: Wiley, 2010.

Andrew Tilin
The Doper Next Door: My Strange and Scandalous Year on Performance-Enhancing Drugs. Berkeley, CA: Counterpoint, 2011.

Ida Walker
Steroids: Pumped Up and Dangerous. Broomall, PA: Mason Crest Publishers, 2012.

Index

A

Academic cheating, 25, 162–169, 170–175

Accidental banned substance ingestion, 23, 119, 143–145

Achilles tendon, 41

Acromegaly, 68, 85–86, 93, 98

ACTN3 gene ("sports gene"), 15

Addiction
cognitive-enhancing drugs, 162–169, 170, 173, 174
nonprofit groups, 95
to "pill lifestyle," 175

Adenosine triphosphate, 88

Aesthetic values of sport, 21, 22–23, 32, 73, 78

African runners, 39, 41–42, 44

Alanine aminotransferase (ALT), 81

Alcohol, 106

American Swimming Magazine, 122–128

Amphetamines, 86, 87, 106, 171
See also Stimulants

Anabolic steroids
body production, 58, 67, 97
danger and bans, 65, 67–68, 74, 75, 81, 96, 97, 99
forms, 83
gene doping as replacement, 14
labs providing, 97, 126, 132
masking agents, 132, 156, 159
names, 82–83, 84, 132
Olympics busts, 22, 73, 84, 106, 132

side effects, 67–68, 83–85, 94
testing methods and timing, 105, 106–107, 130, 132
use by non-athletes, 80, 82–85
use by teens, 82–83, 91, 94

Anadrol, 83

Analgesics, 74, 75, 77

Andersen, Ross, 165

Androstenedione, 67, 84–85

Anemia, 57, 70, 87, 151, 154–155

Animal hormones, 108

Animal testing, 149, 151–152

Anorexia, in cycling training, 47, 50

Anti-aging drugs, 67, 84, 85

Antidepressants, 74

Anti-Doping Denmark, 143–145

Anti-doping organizations, 114, 115, 116, 130, 157–158
See also US Anti-Doping Agency; World Anti-Doping Agency (WADA)

Anti-Doping Research (nonprofit agency), 133

Anti-myostatin drugs, 149–155

Armstrong, Daniel, 148

Armstrong, Lance
admission of PED use, 19, 22, 92, 158
admonishment *vs.* absolution, 19–20, 35, 46
doping quotes, 27
ethics and role-model history, 22, 25
implicated, 49, 66

Ashenden, Michael, 140

S